ISO 9001:2000 Audit Procedures

About the author

Ray Tricker (MSc, IEng, FIIE (elec), FinstM, FIQA, MIRSE) as well as being the Principal Consultant and Managing Director of Herne European Consultancy Ltd – an organisation specialising in Quality, Environment and Safety Management Systems – is also an established Butterworth-Heinemann author (see Reference section). He served with the Royal Corps of Signals (for a total of 37 years) during which time he held various managerial posts culminating in being appointed as the Chief Engineer of NATO ACE COMSEC.

Most of Ray's work since joining Herne has centred on the European Railways. He has held a number of posts with the Union International des Chemins de fer (UIC) (e.g. Quality Manager of the European Train Control System (ETCS), European Union (EU) T500 Review Team Leader, European Rail Traffic Management System (ERTMS) Users Group Project Co-ordinator, HEROE Project Co-ordinator, ERRI Quality Consultant) and currently (as well as writing books for Butterworth-Heinemann and acting as the Technical Author for Leica Microsystems in Cambridge!) he is busy co-ordinating the establishment of a complete Quality Management System for the Association of American Railroads (AAR) Transportation Technology Centre (TTCI) in Pueblo, Colorado, that is aimed at eventually gaining them ISO 9001:2000 certification. Ray is also a member of the Notified Body for the Accreditation of Trans-European High Speed Railways.

To my grandson Kenneth

ISO 9001:2000
Audit Procedures

Ray Tricker

ELSEVIER
BUTTERWORTH
HEINEMANN

AMSTERDAM • BOSTON • HEIDELBERG • LONDON • NEW YORK • OXFORD
PARIS • SAN DIEGO • SAN FRANCISCO • SINGAPORE • SYDNEY • TOKYO

Elsevier Butterworth-Heinemann
Linacre House, Jordan Hill, Oxford OX2 8DP
200 Wheeler Road, Burlington, MA 01803

First published 2002
Reprinted 2003

British Library Cataloguing in Publication Data
A catalogue record for this book is available from the British Library

Library of Congress Cataloguing in Publication Data
A catalogue record for this book is available from the Library of Congress

ISBN 0 7506 5436 8

For information on all Butterworth-Heinemann publications
visit our website at www.bh.com

Composition by Genesis Typesetting, Laser Quay, Rochester, Kent
Printed and bound in Great Britain

Contents

Foreword

One of the requirements of ISO 9001:2000 (Section 8.2.2) is that:

'The organisation shall conduct internal audits at planned intervals to determine whether the quality management system:

a. conforms to the requirements of the ISO 9001:2000 standard and to the quality management system requirements established by the organisation and,

b. is effectively implemented and maintained.'

To meet this requirement, organisations must continually review their system to ensure its continuing suitability and success, reveal defects, danger spots or irregularities, suggest possible improvements, eliminate wastage or loss, check the effectiveness of management at all levels and be sure that managerial objectives and methods are effective and are capable of achieving the desired result. Above all, organisations must be prepared to face up to an audit of their own quality processes and procedures from potential customers and prove to them that their Quality Management System fully meets the recommendations, requirements and specifications of ISO 9001:2000 – and is capable of meeting customer requirements.

The aim of this book, with its audit checklists and explanations, is to assist auditors in completing internal, external and third party audits of **newly implemented** ISO 9001:2000 QMSs, **existing** ISO 9001:1994, ISO 9002:1994 and ISO 9003:1994 compliant Quality Management Systems (QMSs), and **transitional** QMSs.

Preface

ISO 9001:2000 and ISO 9004:2000 have been developed as a *'consistent pair'* of Quality Management System standards, based on eight quality management principles with a common process-orientated structure and harmonised terminology. In contrast to the previous 1994 version of these standards, they are designed to meet the requirements of service industries as well as manufacturers and may be used together or as stand-alone documents. Together, they lay down requirements for incorporating the management of quality into the design, manufacture and delivery of products, services and software.

The idea of a 'consistent pair' of standards was the very core of the revision process and their aligned structure is aimed at encouraging organisations not only to look at their activities from a process standpoint, but also to look beyond certification to a system which will be truly beneficial in improving operational performance. In this respect, ISO 9001:2000 specifies the requirements for a QMS (that can be used by organisations for certification or contractual purposes) whilst ISO 9004:2000 provides guidance aimed at improving an organisation's overall quality performance. ISO 9004:2000 is not, however, meant as a 'guideline for implementing ISO 9001:2000' nor is it intended for certification or contractual use. Supporting both of these standards is a new standard (i.e. ISO 9000:2000) which supersedes ISO 8402:1995 and describes the fundamentals of Quality Management Systems and specifies their terminology.

To achieve its main objectives, ISO 9001:2000 requires manufacturing plants and service industries to possess a **fully auditable Quality Management System** consisting of Quality Policies, Quality Processes, Quality Procedures and Work Instructions. It is this Quality Management System that will provide the auditable proof that the requirements of ISO 9001:2000 have been and are still being met. This book, with its audit checklists and explanations, is designed to assist auditors in completing internal, external and third party audits of ISO 9001:2000 Quality Management Systems. Its checklists may also be used to audit existing ISO 9001:1994, ISO 9002:1994 and ISO 9003:1994 compliant Quality Management Systems.

The book is divided into three parts with the first one describing the requirements of ISO 9001:2000, the second providing background information for auditors and the third containing audit checklists and detailed explanations of the likely documents that will be required by an organisation in order to meet the requirements of ISO 9001:2000.

This book describes methods for completing management reviews and quality audits. It describes how internal audits of the organisation's system are managed, how external audits of the organisation's suppliers are performed and how third party audits may be completed on suppliers, on behalf of an organisation, or as part of a certification requirement for ISO 9001:2000. In totality, this book describes:

- the background to the ISO 9001:2000 standard;
- how ISO 9001:2000 can be used to check an organisation's QMS;
- how internal and external audits should be completed (e.g. audit plan, supplier evaluation, surveillance or quality audit visits);
- how quality assurance can affect the product throughout its lifecycle;
- the manufacturer's, supplier's and purchaser's responsibilities;
- the benefits and costs of quality assurance;
- QMS requirements, principles and determinates;
- the type of documentation an organisation needs to satisfy the requirements of ISO 9001:2000;

and then in a series of separate sections:

- lists the headings of ISO 9001:2000;
- provides a comparison between ISO 9001:2000 and ISO 9001:1994;
- provides a counter-comparison between ISO 9001:1994 and ISO 9001:2000;
- shows a comparison between the headings of ISO 9001:2000 and those contained in the previous Committee Drafts (CD1 and CD2), the Draft International Standard (DIS) and the Final Draft International Standard (FDIS);
- provides a complete index to ISO 9001:2000;
- provides a crosscheck between the requirements of ISO 9001:2000 and that of any previous QMS certified to ISO 9001:1994;
- lists the likely documentation that an organisation would need to meet the individual requirements of ISO 9001:2000;
- provides an audit check sheet against ISO 9001:2000;
- provides stage audit check sheets;
- provides additional audit checks that can be used to check existing (e.g. ISO 9001:1994) QMSs against ISO 9001:2000;
- provides examples of the main audit forms required to comply with ISO 9001:2000.

The book also provides a list of all the main acronyms and abbreviations associated with quality management together with a detailed glossary of terms used in quality.

For convenience (and in order to reduce the number of equivalent or similar terms) the following, unless otherwise stated, are considered interchangeable terms within this book:

- product – hardware, software, service or processed material;
- organisation – manufacturer and/or service provider.

1 BACKGROUND TO THE ISO 9001:2000 STANDARD

During the last few years it had been recognised that the 1994 version of the ISO 9000 series (i.e. ISO 9001:1994, ISO 9002:1994 and ISO 9003:1994) was far too orientated towards manufacturing and that there was a need to revise the existing structure of the standard to try and suit **all** organisations, no matter their type or size.

Under existing international agreement, all International Standards have to be reinspected, 5 years after publication, for their continued applicability. In accordance with this agreement, the International Standards Organisation (ISO) contacted more than 1,000 users and organisations for their views on ISO 9000:1994 using a questionnaire covering:

- problems with the existing standards;
- requirements for new/revised standards;
- possible harmonisation and interoperability between quality management, environmental management and health and safety standards.

1.1 The revision process

The revision process was the responsibility of ISO Technical Committee (TC) 176 and was conducted on the basis of consensus among quality and industry experts nominated by ISO member bodies, and representing all interested parties. Initial specifications and goals were established following extensive user surveys and these were followed by a user verification and validation process to ensure that the standards produced would actually meet the requirements of the user.

The programme of work was as follows:

4th quarter 1997	1st Working Draft (WD1) for use by TC-176
1st quarter 1998	2nd Working Draft (WD2) for use by TC-176
2nd quarter 1998	3rd Working Draft (WD3) for use by TC-176
July 1998	Committee Draft (CD1) issued for ballot
February 1999	Committee Draft (CD2) issued for ballot
November 1999	Draft International Standard (DIS) for comment and vote by Member Countries (see note)
September 2000	Publication of Final Draft International Standard (FDIS)
December 2000	Publication of International Standard (ISO)

Note: Once Draft International Standards have been adopted by the technical committees they are then circulated to member bodies for voting. Publication as an International Standard then requires a two-thirds majority of the votes.

In the words of the International Standards Organisation (ISO) the main reason for the year 2000 revision to the ISO 9000 standards was '*to give users the opportunity to add value to their activities and to improve their performance continually by focussing on the major processes within the organisation*'.

The aims of the revision process were to:

- guarantee the effectiveness (but not necessarily the efficiency) of the organisation;
- make sure the standards were applicable to all types of organisations;
- make the language used in the revised standards simpler, more user-friendly, and with less manufacturing bias;

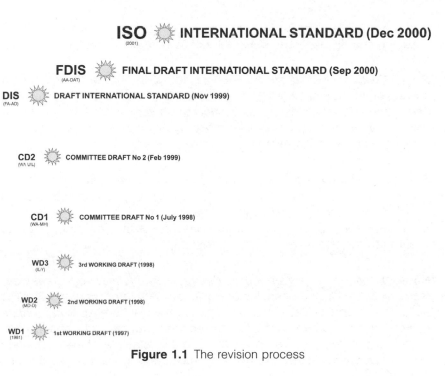

Figure 1.1 The revision process

- make the new standards so that they were equally appropriate to all sectors, including service providers;
- produce standards that would minimize any potential costs during a smooth transition.

1.2   The main changes

The new standards have taken into account previous experience with quality management system standards such as the original BS 5750 series, the 1987 and 1994 editions of ISO 9000, as well as emerging generic management systems. This has resulted in a closer alignment of quality management systems with the needs of organisations better reflecting the way organisations run their business activities.

Virtually all of the requirements from the previous 1994 standard have been included in the revised ISO 9001:2000 standard but with clearer definition and the inclusion of a lot of 'shalls' as opposed to 'coulds' and 'shoulds'. The main changes have been that the new standard:

- is centred around a process-orientated structure with a more logical sequence of contents;

- includes a requirement for the organisation to monitor information on customer satisfaction as a measure of system performance;

Note: '*Customer satisfaction*' is recognised as one of the driving criteria for any organisation. In order to evaluate if the product meets customer needs and expectations, it is necessary to monitor the extent of customer satisfaction. Improvements can be made by taking action to address any identified issues and concerns.

- gives considerable emphasis on higher management issues (such as the need for defined (and auditable) quality targets and the need to include supporting activities within the system);
- includes a continual improvement process as an important step to enhance the quality management system;

Note: '*Continual improvement is the process focused on continually increasing the effectiveness and/or efficiency of the organisation to fulfil its policies and objectives. Continual improvement (where 'continual' highlights that an improvement process requires progressive consolidation steps) responds to the growing needs and expectations of the customers and ensures a dynamic evolution of the quality management system*' (ISO TC 176).

- provides (in ISO 9004:2000) an additional concept of organisational self-assessment as a driver for improvement (further emphasising the need to monitor customer satisfaction);
- establishes measurable objectives at relevant functions and levels (monitoring of information of customer satisfaction as a measure of system performance);
- lays increased emphasis on the role of top management, including a commitment to the development and improvement of the quality management system, consideration of legal and regulatory requirements, and establishment of measurable objectives at relevant functions and levels (see also 1.3.4);
- extends measurements to include system, processes, and product;
- increases attention to resource availability;
- emphasises the need to determine training effectiveness;
- considers the benefits and needs of all interested parties;
- assures consistency between quality management system requirements and guidelines;
- promotes the use of generic quality management principles by organisations (and enhancement of their compatibility with ISO 14001);
- significantly reduces the amount of documentation required;

- includes terminology changes and improvements that allow easier interpretation;
- provides increased compatibility with the environmental management system standard;
- makes specific reference to quality management principles;
- meets the need for more user-friendly documents;
- provides measures for the analysis of collected data concerning the performance of an organisation's quality management system.

1.3   Key changes

1.3.1   Requirements

The main difference between ISO 9001:2000 and the previous version of the standard is that the 20 elements contained in section four of ISO 9001:1994 have now been replaced by four sections covering the management of resources, the quality of the product, the maintenance of quality records and the requirement for continual improvement.

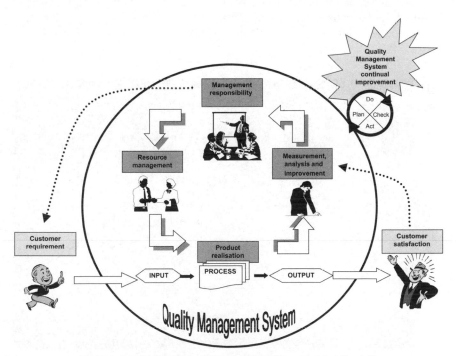

Figure 1.2 ISO 9001:2000 Quality Management System

1.3.2   Revised title

Each of the three main standards (i.e. ISO 9000:2000, ISO 9001:2000 and ISO 9004:2000) now have a revised title, which no longer includes the term '*quality assurance*'. This has been done in order to reflect the fact that the QMS requirements specified in these standards address the quality assurance of a product as well as customer satisfaction.

1.3.3   Consistent pair of standards

ISO 9001:2000 and ISO 9004:2000 have been developed as a '*consistent pair*' of QMS standards, based on eight quality management principles with a common process-orientated structure and harmonised terminology. They are designed to be used together, or may be used as stand-alone documents.

The idea of a 'consistent pair' of standards is the very core of the revision process. The aligned structure of ISO 9001:2000 and ISO 9004:2000 is aimed at encouraging organisations not only to look at their activities from a process standpoint, but also to look beyond certification to a system which will be truly beneficial in improving operational performance.

Whilst ISO 9001:2000 specifies the requirements for a QMS (that can be used by organisations for certification or contractual purposes), ISO 9004:2000 provides guidance aimed at improving an organisation's overall quality performance. ISO 9004:2000 is not, however, meant as a

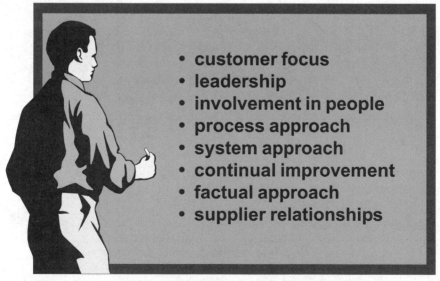

- **customer focus**
- **leadership**
- **involvement in people**
- **process approach**
- **system approach**
- **continual improvement**
- **factual approach**
- **supplier relationships**

Figure 1.3 The eight quality management principles

'guideline for implementing ISO 9001:2000' nor is it intended for certification or contractual use.

Both of the standards are based on eight quality management principles, which reflect best management practices.

These eight principles are:

- customer focused organisation;
- leadership;
- involvement of people;
- process approach;
- system approach to management;
- continual improvement;
- factual approach to decision making;
- mutually beneficial supplier relationship.

One specific change to ISO 9001:2000 and ISO 9004:2000 that was brought about late in the day concerned the usage of the term 'product'. During the Committee Draft stages, it became apparent that there was a need to have a single word that described an organisation's output as well as the service that it provided. Consequently in the new standards, 'product' has been defined as '*a system of activities, which uses resources to transform inputs into outputs*' and there are four agreed generic product categories, namely:

- hardware;
- software;
- services;
- processed materials.

Note: Further details of the Transition Planning Guidance are available on BSI's website at http://www.bsi.org.uk/iso-tc176-sc2.

1.3.4 Top management

Top management is a new term in ISO 9001:2000 and is defined as '*a person or group of people who direct and control an organisation at the highest level*'.

In essence the standard is now no longer dealing with a Quality Management System but more of a management system that is to be used by the whole organisation. However, no organisation can function effectively without direction from top management, but in order to know that direction they will need to have at their disposal a wide range of information so they can provide a vision for the future. One of the main pieces of information they will need to have readily available is the needs and expectations of their customers, as well as knowing the regulatory and legal requirements that are applicable to the organisation. This will enable top management to know what they need to do within the organisation to achieve customer satisfaction.

Management then needs to be able to show the workforce what the purpose of the organisation is, the perceived values of the organisation and their attitude and actions towards the customers. Through the mission and policy statements, management should try to produce unity within the organisation by enabling the staff to see clearly what the organisation is striving to achieve.

In the past, an organisation's Quality Policy was seen more as a piece of paper signed by a senior member of staff rather than an objective. Now the policy will need to show a commitment to improvement, which will be measured throughout the organisation to make sure that the policy provides a framework for the setting of the objectives, and is communicated and understood throughout the organisation.

Once the policies have been set, policy objectives will need to be established. These should be applicable to the various activities within the organisation, and take into account the various functions of the organisation and how these fit into the strategic framework.

Top management should engender a culture within the organisation that makes sure that all staff know what their objectives are and the relevance and importance of how staff do can affect the overall objectives of the organisation. Through having a caring and open culture, the morale and motivation of the workforce will be improved and as a consequence, products and services supplied will improve as will customer satisfaction. They will also need to take into consideration the interested parties of the organisation (see also 1.5).

1.3.5   The process model

The whole concept of ISO 9001:2000 now revolves round a systematic process approach which uses eight quality management principles reflecting best practice which are designed to enable a continual improvement of the business, its overall efficiency and be capable of responding to customer needs and expectations.

The eight principles contained in ISO 9001:2000 are of primary concern to an organisation, as they will affect an organisation's overall approach to quality. They are:

1.   *Customer focused organisation*
Organisations depend on their customers and therefore should understand current and future customer needs. They should meet customer requirements and should strive to exceed customer expectations.

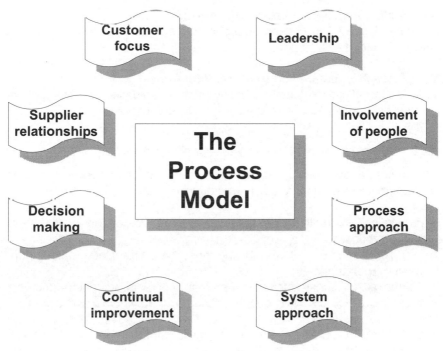

Figure 1.4 The process model

2. Leadership
Leaders establish unity of purpose, direction, and the internal environment of their organisation. They create the environment in which people can become fully involved in achieving the organisation's objectives.

3. Involvement of people
People at all levels are the essence of an organisation and their full involvement enables their abilities to be used for the organisation's benefit.

4. Process approach
A desired result is achieved more efficiently when related resources and activities are managed as a process.

5. System approach to management
Identifying, understanding and managing a system of inter-related processes for a given objective contributes to the effectiveness and efficiency of the organisation.

6. Continual improvement
Continual improvement is a permanent objective of any organisation.

7.   *Factual approach to decision making*

Effective decisions are based on the logical and intuitive analysis of data and information.

8.   *Mutually beneficial supplier relationships*

Mutually beneficial relationships between an organisation and its suppliers enhance the ability of both organisations to create value.

1.4   Benefits of the revised standards

There are many, quite major benefits because of the revised quality management systems standard structure, such as:

- its applicability to all product categories, in all sectors and to all sizes of organisations;
- being simpler to use, clearer in language, readily translatable, and more easily understandable;
- having a significant reduction in the amount of required documentation;
- providing a link between quality management systems and organisational processes;
- providing a natural move towards improved organisational performance;
- covering the requirement for continual improvement and customer satisfaction;
- its increased compatibility with other management systems such as ISO 14000;
- providing a consistent basis to address the needs and interests of organisations in specific sectors (e.g. medical devices, telecommunications, automotive, etc.);
- the concept of the consistent pair (ISO 9001 covering the requirements and ISO 9004 for going beyond the requirements in order to further improve the performance of the organisation);
- considering the needs of and benefits to all interested parties.

1.5   Other benefits

As shown below, the benefits of an organisation implementing an ISO 9001:2000 culture are far-reaching.

1.5.1   Customers

Customers and users will benefit by receiving products that:

- conform to the requirements;
- are dependable and reliable;

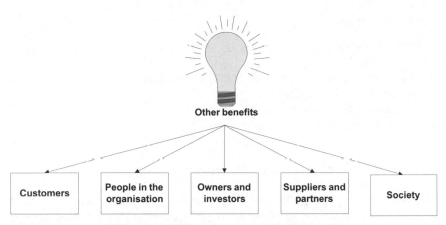

Figure 1.5 Other benefits of ISO 9001:2000

- are available when needed;
- are maintainable.

1.5.2   People in the organisation

People in the organisation will benefit by:

- better working conditions;
- increased job satisfaction;
- improved health and safety;
- improved morale;
- improved stability of employment.

1.5.3   Owners and investors

Owners and investors will benefit by:

- increased return on investment;
- improved operational results;
- increased market share;
- increased profits.

1.5.4   Suppliers and partners

Suppliers and partners will benefit by:

- stability;
- growth;
- partnership and mutual understanding.

1.5.5   Society

Society will benefit by:

- fulfilment of legal and regulatory requirements;
- improved health and safety;
- reduced environmental impact;
- increased security.

1.6   Permissible exclusions

The text of ISO 9001:2000 has been made more generic than the 1994 version in order to be applicable to different types of product and to organisations of different sizes. Due to this generic nature, however, it may be that some industrial or commercial sectors will identify additional requirements to attend to their specific needs.

Equally, some of the requirements may not apply to all organisations and in this respect ISO allows for the exclusion of some requirements. These exclusions are limited to Section 7 ('Product Realisation'), and requirements can **only** be left out if it can be shown that they do not affect the organisation's ability to provide a product which meets customer and applicable statutory/regulatory requirements.

1.7   Transition period

The 1994 ISO 9000 family of quality standards contained well over 27 standards and documents and this caused quite a lot of concern (not to mention confusion!) over the years. Thankfully the year 2000 quality management system standards now only consist of three primary standards, i.e. ISO 9000, ISO 9001 and ISO 9004 supported by a number of technical reports.

To the maximum extent possible, the key points in the other 1994 standards and documents (and sector-specific needs) have been integrated into the three primary standards. Then over the next few years the other standards and documents from the ISO 9000 family will either be withdrawn, transferred to other Technical Committees, or replaced by technical reports, technical specifications or brochures (with the exception of ISO 10012 'Quality Assurance for Measuring Equipment', which will remain as an international standard).

Although the year 2000 publications now supersede corresponding 1994 versions of the standards, previous (i.e. accredited) certification to the 1994 editions will be recognised up to 3 years following publication of the revised standards (i.e. until December 2003). Organisations may choose to continue or even seek new certification/registration to the 1994 versions of ISO 9001, ISO 9002, and ISO 9003. But any certificates issued or renewed will only remain valid until December 2003.

Note: Although upgrading an organisation's QMS to ISO 9001:2000 will be fairly simple if that organisation is already certified to ISO 9001:1994, the impact on organisations who are currently only registered to ISO 9002:1994 and 9003:1994 (i.e. organisations **not** involved in the design and manufacture of a product) will probably be more difficult!

Following consultation between ISO/TC 176, the International Accreditation Forum (IAF) and the ISO/Committee of Conformity Assessment (CASCO), a joint communiqué has been issued which includes the following statements:

- *'Accredited certificates to the new ISO 9001 shall not be granted until the publication of ISO 9001:2000 as an International Standard'.*
- *'Certification/registration body assessments to the latest draft of the new standard may begin prior to the publication of the ISO 9001:2000 International Standard'.*
- *'ISO 9001:2000 will require auditors and other relevant certification/ registration body personnel to demonstrate new competencies'.*
- *'Certification/registration bodies will need to take particular care in defining the scope of certificates issued to ISO 9001:2000, and the "permissible exclusions" to the requirements of that standard'.*
- *'Certificates issued to ISO 9001:1994, ISO 9002:1994 or ISO 9003:1994 shall have a maximum validity of 3 years from the date of publication of ISO 9001:2000'.*

However, although organisations already registered to the 1994 standard will have up to 3 years following publication of the ISO 9001:2000 in which to re-certify, it is strongly recommended that, if you are one of these organisations, you make a start on the transition to the new standard as soon as possible!

1.8 Cost

'An effective QMS should be designed to satisfy the purchaser's conditions, requirements and expectations whilst serving to protect the organisation's best interests' (ISO 9004: 2000).

   In practice, Quality Management Systems can be very expensive to install and operate, particularly if inadequate quality assurance and quality control methods were previously used. If the purchaser requires consistent quality he must pay for it, regardless of the specification or order which the organisation has accepted. However, against this expenditure

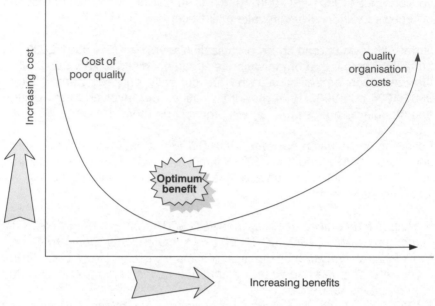

Figure 1.6 Quality Management System costs

must always be offset by savings in rework, scrapped material and general problems arising from lack of quality.

From an organisation's point of view there is a business requirement to obtain and maintain the desired quality at an optimum cost. The following represent some of the additional expenses that can be incurred:

- implementation and maintenance of an organised document control system throughout the organisation;
- training for the quality assurance team;
- salaries for the quality assurance team, planners, quality supervisors, calibration/test equipment staff and Quality Managers;
- visits by the quality assurance staff to other organisations, subcontractors and the eventual consumer, for evaluation and audit of their facilities and products;
- test equipment of a recognised type, standard and quality; regularly maintained and calibrated by an accredited calibration centre;
- better storage facilities.

Note: With an effective QMS in place, the supplier will achieve increased profitability and market share and the purchaser can expect reduced costs, improved product fitness for role, increased satisfaction and, above all, growth in confidence.

The cost of implementing any necessary changes in order to meet the new requirements of ISO 9001:2000 will obviously vary from one organisation to another, depending on various factors such as the actual state of implementation of the Quality Management System, the size and complexity of the organisation, the attitude and commitment of the top management, etc. It is expected that the benefits to all organisations, however, will far outweigh eventual costs associated with the transition and any additional costs should be considered as a 'value-added investment'.

1.9 The ISO 9000:2000 family of standards

The ISO 9000:2000 family of standards consists of three primary standards supported by a number of technical reports. These are:

Figure 1.7 The ISO 9000:2000 family

1.9.1   ISO 9000:2000

ISO 9000:2000

Quality Management Systems – Fundamentals and vocabulary (*superseding ISO 8402:1995 'Quality Management and Quality Assurance – Vocabulary' and ISO 9000–1:1994 'Quality Management and Quality Assurance Standards – Guidelines for selection and use'*).

ISO 9000:2000 now includes a description of the basic approach to quality management as well as including a revised vocabulary to reflect the usage of new and revised terms and associated definitions contained in ISO 9001:2000 and ISO 9004:2000.

The development of ISO 9000:2000 was completed in parallel with ISO 9001:2000, ISO 9004:2000, the future ISO 14001 standard for environmental management and all other existing and planned management standards so as to, hopefully, ensure a harmonised approach to standardisation.

ISO 9000:2000 also includes a revision of the current ISO 8402:1995 'Quality Management and Quality Assurance – Vocabulary' standard, provides a more formal approach to the definition of terms, specifies terminology for QMSs and will assist:

- those concerned with enhancing the mutual understanding of the terminology used in quality management (e.g. suppliers, customers, regulators);
- internal or external auditors, regulators, certification and/or registration bodies;
- developers of related standards.

Following publication of this standard, ISO 8402:1995 has been withdrawn.

1.9.2   ISO 9001:2000

ISO 9001:2000

Quality Management Systems – Requirements *(superseding ISO 9001:1994 'Quality Systems – Model for quality assurance in design, development, production, installation and servicing', ISO 9002:1994 'Quality Systems – Model for quality assurance in production, installation and servicing' and ISO 9003:1994 'Quality Systems – Model for quality assurance in final inspection and test').*

The current ISO 9001:1994, ISO 9002:1994 and ISO 9003:1994 standards have now been consolidated into a single revised ISO 9001:2000 standard. Organisations that have previously used ISO 9002:1994 and ISO 9003:1994 will be allowed to be certified to ISO 9001:2000 through a '*reduction in scope*' of the standard's requirements by omitting requirements that do not apply to their particular organisation.

ISO 9001:2000 is focused towards '*providing confidence, as a result of demonstration, in product conformance to established requirements*' and includes a section entitled '*permissible exclusions*'. This section allows organisations to formally '*exclude*' certain non-applicable requirements of the standard, yet still claim conformance to it. However, only those organisations that can **prove** that the nature of their products, customers and/or the applicable regulatory requirements do not need to meet the full requirements of ISO 9001:2000 are allowed these exclusions. For example, organisations whose products require no design activities (and who would have previously sought ISO 9002:1994 certification) can now claim to be in compliance with ISO 9001:2000 by excluding the requirements for design and development.

With the publication of ISO 9001:2000, there is now, therefore, a single quality management '**requirements**' standard that is applicable to all organisations, products and services. It is the only standard that can be used for the certification of a QMS and its generic requirements can be used by **any** organisation to:

- address customer satisfaction;
- meet customer and applicable regulatory requirements;
- enable internal and external parties (including certification bodies) to assess the organisation's ability to meet these customer and regulatory requirements.

For certification purposes, organisations will now have to possess a documented management system that takes the inputs and transforms them into targeted outputs. Something that effectively:

- says what they are going to do;
- does what they have said they are going to do;
- keeps records of everything that they do – especially when things go wrong.

The basic process to achieve these targeted outputs will encompass:

- the client's requirements;
- the inputs from management and staff;
- documented controls for any activities that are needed to produce the finished article;
- and, of course, delivering a product or service, which satisfies the customer's original requirements.

The adoption of a QMS has to be a strategic decision of any organisation and the design and implementation of their QMS will be influenced by its varying needs, objectives, products provided, processes employed and the size and structure of that organisation. As ISO are quick to point out, however, it is not the intention of ISO 9001:2000 to insist on a uniform structure to QMSs, or uniformity of documentation and the QMS requirements specified in this standard should always be viewed as complementary to product technical requirements.

1.9.2.1   ISO 9001:2000's generic processes

The ISO 9001:2000 standard is the only standard within the 2000 edition to which an organisation can be certified. It includes all the key points from the previous 20 elements of ISO 9001:1994, but integrates them into four major generic business processes, namely:

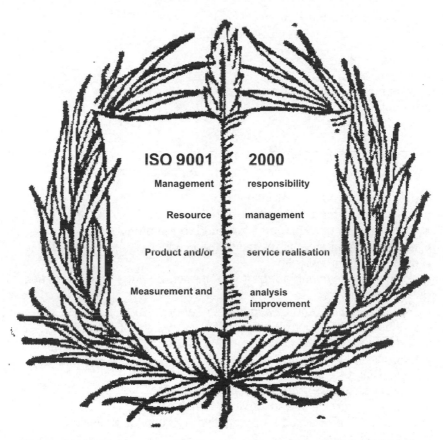

Figure 1.8 The four major generic business processes of ISO 9001:2000

1. *Management responsibility*
Policy, objectives, planning, system review:

- management commitment;
- customer focus;
- quality policy;
- quality objectives;
- quality management system planning;
- responsibility, authority and communication;
- management representative;
- internal communication;
- management review;
- review input;
- review output.

2. Resource management
Human resources, information, facilities:

- provision of resources;
- human resources;
- competence, awareness and training;
- infrastructure;
- work environment.

3. Product realisation
Customer, design, purchasing, production, calibration:

- planning of product realisation;
- customer-related processes;
- determination of requirements related to the product;
- review of requirements related to the product;
- customer communication;
- design and development planning (inputs, outputs, review, verification and validation);
- control of design and development changes;
- purchasing;
- purchasing process;
- purchasing information;
- verification of purchased product;
- production and service provision;
- control of production and service provision;
- validation of processes for production and service provision;
- identification and traceability;
- customer property;
- preservation of product;
- control of monitoring and measuring devices.

4. Measurement, analysis and improvement
Audit, process/product control, improvement:

- monitoring and measurement;
- customer satisfaction;
- internal audit;
- monitoring and measurement of processes;
- monitoring and measurement of product;
- control of non-conforming product;
- analysis of data;
- improvement;
- continual improvement;
- corrective action;
- preventive action;

1.9.2.2   Brief summary of ISO 9001:2000 requirements

ISO 9001:2000 consists of eight sections which are summarised below.
Note: For a more complete description please see *ISO 9001:2000 for Small Businesses* by Ray Tricker from Butterworth-Heinemann's *ISO 9000:2000* series.

Figure 1.9 ISO 9001:2000 for Small Businesses

1.9.2.3   Section 1 – Scope

This is a short section explaining what the standard covers.

1.9.2.4   Section 2 – Normative reference

Another short section which contains details of other standards that form a **mandatory** input to ISO 9001:2000. In this instance the only reference is ISO 9000:2000 'Quality Management Systems – Fundamentals and vocabulary'.

1.9.2.5   Section 3 – Terms and definitions

The third section explains how the standard is based on a supply chain concept as shown in Figure 1.10.

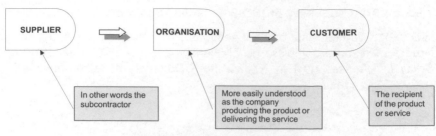

Figure 1.10 The supply chain

1.9.2.6   Section 4 – Quality Management System

This basically states that an organisation **shall** have a documented QMS that defines the processes necessary to ensure that the product conforms to customer requirements. This QMS must be implemented, maintained and, most importantly, continually improved by the organisation.

This section also clearly states the types of documentation required to comply with the standard, as follows:

- **Quality Manual** – the main policy document that establishes the organisation's QMS and how it meets the requirements of ISO 9001:2000;

QMS – Quality Model

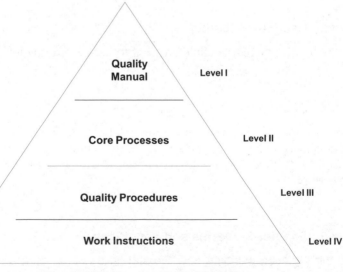

Figure 1.11 Documentation hierarchy

- **Core Processes** – business processes that describe the activities required to implement the QMS and to meet the policy requirements made in the Quality Manual;
- **Quality Procedures** – a description of the method by which quality system activities are managed;
- **Work Instructions** – a description of how a specific task is carried out.

Note: The extent of the QMS documentation (which may be in any form or type of medium) is dependent on the:

- size and type of the organisation;
- complexity and interaction of the processes;
- competency of personnel.

1.9.2.7   Section 5 – Management responsibility

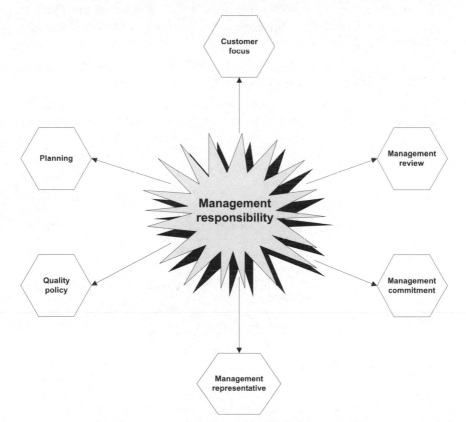

Figure 1.12 Section 5 – Management responsibility

This section contains the majority of the old ISO 9001:1994 management responsibility and quality requirements all rolled together. It is broken down into the following subclauses that cover the requirements for:

- **Management commitment** – top (i.e. senior) management committing, fully, to the development and improvement of the QMS (without their commitment the system will fall at the first hurdle);
- **Customer focus** – determining, fully understanding and documenting customer requirements; ensuring compliance with identified statutory legislation (e.g. EC Directives, other national and international standards, etc.);
- **Quality policy** – ensuring that it is appropriate for the purpose, understood by everyone and reviewed for continued suitability;
- **Planning** – clearly stating management's quality objectives and policy on quality in an established, fully documented, QMS;
- **Management representative** – appointing someone (or some people) to be responsible for the implementation and improvement of the organisation's QMS;
- **Management review** – carrying out regular reviews of the QMS to ensure it continues to function correctly (and to identify areas for improvement).

1.9.2.8   Section 6 – Resource management

This section covers resources with regard to training, induction, responsibilities, working environment, equipment requirements, maintenance, etc.

Figure 1.13 Section 6 – Resource management

It is broken down into the following subsections that cover the requirements for:

- **Provision of resources** – identifying the resources required to implement and improve the processes that make up the QMS;
- **Human resources** – assigning personnel with regard to competency, education, training, skill and/or experience;
- **Infrastructure** – identifying, providing and maintaining the required facilities (e.g. workspace), equipment (hardware and software) and supporting services to achieve conformity of product;
- **Work environment** – identifying and managing the work environment (e.g. health and safety, ambient conditions, etc.).

1.9.2.9 Section 7 – Product realisation

This section absorbs most of the 20 elements of the old ISO 9000:1994 standard, including process control, purchasing, handling and storage, and measuring devices. This section is broken down into a number of subsections that cover the requirements for:

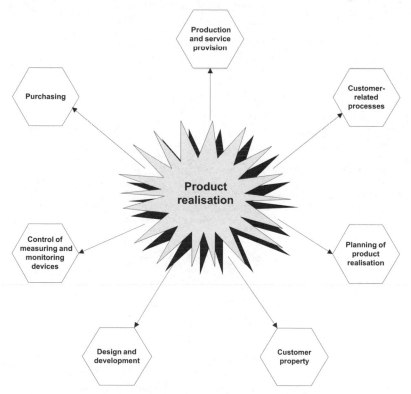

Figure 1.14 Section 7 – Product realisation

- **Planning of realisation processes** – clearly defining and documenting the processes used to ensure reliable and consistent products (e.g. verification and validation activities, criteria for acceptability and quality records, etc.);
- **Customer-related processes** – identifying customer, product, legal and design requirements;
- **Design and development** – controlling the design process (e.g. design inputs, outputs, review, verification, validation and change control);
- **Purchasing** – having documented processes for the selection and control of suppliers and the control of purchases that affect the quality of the finished product or service;
- **Production and service provision** – having documented instructions that control the manufacture of a product or delivery of a service;
- **Customer property** – identifying, verifying, protecting and maintaining customer property provided for use or incorporation with the product;
- **Control of measuring and monitoring devices** – their control, calibration and protection.

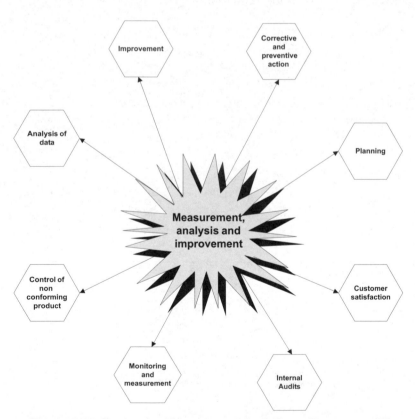

Figure 1.15 Section 8 – Measurement, analysis and improvement

1.9.2.10   Section 8 – Measurement, analysis and improvement

This section absorbs the former inspection and measurement control sections of ISO 9001:1994. It includes requirements for:

- **Planning** – defining the requirements for measurement analysis and improvement (including statistical analysis);
- **Customer satisfaction** – monitoring customer satisfaction/dissatisfaction as a measurement and improvement of the QMS;
- **Internal audits** – conducting periodic internal audits to confirm continued conformity with ISO 9001:2000;
- **Measurement and monitoring of processes and product** – defining processes to monitor the performance of the QMS and the products and services delivered by the organisation;
- **Nonconformity** – controlling nonconformity and its rectification;
- **Data analysis** – collecting and analysing statistical data obtained from the organisation's measuring and monitoring activities to find areas of improvement;
- **improvement** – planning for continual improvement of the QMS;
- **Corrective and preventive action** – having available procedures to address corrective and preventive action.

1.9.2.11   Relationship between ISO 9001:2000 and ISO 14001

ISO 9001:2000 is intended to be compatible with other management system standards, in particular those relating to environmental management, occupational health and safety, and financial management

Whilst ISO 9001:2000 does not, however, include any requirements that are specific to any of these other management systems, it does, nevertheless, allow an organisation to align and integrate its own QMS with other (related) management system requirements. In some cases, it may even be possible for an organisation to adapt its existing management system(s) in order to establish a QMS that complies with the requirements of ISO 9001:2000.

The anticipated publication date for the joint Quality Management System and Environmental Management System auditing standard (ISO 19011) is planned for 2002 and will merge the current ISO 10011 Parts 1, 2 and 3 with ISO 14010, 14011, and 14012.

1.9.3   ISO 9004:2000

Quality Management Systems – Guidelines for performance improvement *(superseding ISO 9004–1:1994 'Quality Management and Quality System Elements – Guidelines).*

ISO 9004:2000

ISO 9004:2000 provides guidance on QMSs, including the processes that are required for continual improvement and, ultimately, customer satisfaction. The guidance should be viewed as generic and with the overall aim of being applicable to all organisations, regardless of the type, size and the product provided.

The standard is focused towards providing '*benefits for all interested parties through sustained customer satisfaction*'. ISO 9004:2000 also includes the requirements of ISO 9001:2000 in text boxes inserted in appropriate places (which means perhaps that organisations only need to purchase ISO 9004:2000 and not both standards – how strange of ISO to miss this: funny old world!).

ISO 9004:2000 now includes an annex giving guidance on 'self-assessment' to enable an organisation to check the status of their QMS. This will prove very useful for organisations who are considering applying for ISO 9001:2000 certification, but are unsure what additional quality documentation will be required.

ISO 9004:2000 is also aimed at improving an organisation's overall quality performance and provides a stepping stone to Total Quality Management (TQM). In the words of the standard:

> '*ISO 9004:2000 is designed to go beyond quality management requirements and provide organisations with guidelines for perform-ance improvement through sustained customer satisfaction. In doing so it:*
>
> - *provides guidance to management on the application and use of a QMS to improve an organisation's overall performance;*
> - *is recommended as a guide for organisations whose manage-ment wishes to move beyond the minimum requirements of ISO 9001 in pursuit of increased performance improvement ISO 9004 is not intended as guidance for compliance with ISO 9001;*

- *defines the minimum QMS requirements needed to achieve customer satisfaction by meeting specified product requirements;*
- *can be also be used by an organisation to demonstrate its capability to meet customer requirements'.*

Note: This international standard is **not** a guideline for implementing ISO 9001 and is **not** intended for certification, regulatory or contractual use.

For completeness, a new standard is being written to assist auditing systems against ISO 9001:2000; this will be ISO 19011.

Note: All of the other standards and documents within the ISO 9000:1994 family that were submitted for formal review by ISO member bodies during the committee stages will probably be withdrawn in the near future.

1.9.4   ISO 19011

ISO 19011

Guidelines on auditing quality and environmental management systems *(to supersede ISO 10011–1:1990 'Guidelines for Auditing Quality Systems – Auditing', ISO 10011–2:1991 'Guidelines for Auditing Quality Systems – Qualification criteria for quality system auditors', ISO 10011–3:1991 'Guidelines for Auditing Quality Systems – Management of audit programmes', as well as ISO 14010:1996 'Guidelines for Environmental Auditing – General principles', ISO 14011:1996 'Guidelines for Environmental Auditing – Audit procedures – Auditing of environmental management systems' and ISO 14012:1996 'Guidelines for Environmental Auditing – Qualification criteria for environmental auditors').*

This new standard will provide guidance on managing and conducting environmental and quality audits. Currently this standard is at the Committee Draft stage, but it is scheduled for publication during the 4th quarter 2001.

2 BACKGROUND NOTES FOR AUDITORS

One of the requirements of ISO 9001:2000 (Section 8.2.2) is that:

> '*The organisation shall conduct internal audits at planned intervals to determine whether the quality management system:*
>
> a. *conforms to the requirements of the ISO 9001:2000 standard and to the quality management system requirements established by the organisation and,*
> b. *is effectively implemented and maintained.*'

In order to meet and satisfy this requirement, organisations must continually review their Quality Management System (QMS):

- to ensure its continuing suitability and success;
- to reveal defects, danger spots or irregularities;
- to suggest possible improvements;
- to eliminate wastage or loss;
- to check the effectiveness of management at all levels;
- to ensure that managerial objectives and methods are effective and are capable of achieving the desired result.

Above all, organisations must be prepared to face up to an audit of their quality processes and procedures from potential customers and prove to them that their QMS fully meets the recommendations, requirements and specifications of ISO 9001:2000 and their promises made regarding product and/or service quality.

Whilst the previous 1994 editions of ISO 9000 were primarily concerned with manufacturers, ISO 9001:2000 being a process-orientated requirements standard is equally applicable to service industries and manufacturing plants. With the publication of the new ISO 9000 series, therefore, auditors, whether external or internal, will have to demonstrate their competence not only on the structure, content and terminology of the revised standards, but also on the underlying quality management principles. The revised standards will require that auditors be able to understand the organisation's activities and processes and appropriately audit against the requirements of the standard in relation to the organisation's objectives. As a minimum, auditors must demonstrate competency in:

- the requirements of ISO 9001:2000;
- the concepts and terminology of ISO 9000:2000;
- the eight quality management principles, namely:
  - customer focus,
  - leadership,
  - involvement of people,
  - process approach,
  - system approach to management,
  - continual improvement,
  - factual approach to decision making, and
  - mutually beneficial supplier relationships;
- having a general understanding of the performance improvement guidelines of ISO 9004:2000;
- familiarity with the latest draft of the auditing guidance standard (ISO 19011).

2.1 Purpose of an audit

The primary purpose of an audit is to enable organisations to evaluate their process management systems, determine deficiencies, and generate cost effective and efficient solutions. An audit is performed to check practice against procedure, and to thoroughly document any differences. It is used to measure an organisation's ability '*to do what it says it is going to do*'.

2.2 Types of audit

There are several types of audit that can be completed under the general umbrella of '*audits measuring conformance with ISO 9001:2000*' such as:

Quality System Audits An overall measurement of an organisation's capability to meet the requirements of ISO 9001:2000.

Management Audits   Verification that an organisation's strategic plans accurately reflect their business objectives and the requirements of the intended market.

Process Audits   Verification that a process is capable of consistently providing a product or service that meets agreed requirements.

Procedural Audits   Verification that documented practices are sufficient to ensure the implementation of approved policies and are capable of controlling the organisation's operations.

System Audits   Verification that an organisation's documented management system not only complies with the requirements of ISO 9001:2000, but that it ensures effective and complete control of all of the organisation's activities and achieves its stated objectives.

Product/Service Audits   Verification that an organisation's plans and proposals for supplying a product or service will ensure that that product or service fully meets specified requirements.

2.3   Audit categories

Whilst the common aim of all audits is to establish that an organisation's documented policies, processes and procedures, when implemented, are fit for their purpose and satisfy the needs of those who require them, the actual type of audit will depend on whether it is a First, Second or Third Party Audit. These are the three main types of audit associated with ISO 9001:2000 and are used as follows:

First Party   Audits of an organisation, or parts of an organisation, by personnel employed by that organisation. These audits are usually referred to as Internal Audits.

Second Party   Audits carried out by customers upon their suppliers and completed by an organisation independent of the organisation being audited. These audits are usually referred to as External Audits or Vendor Audits.

Note: As all organisations are '*suppliers*' of one sort or another this can also, in some cases, be an audit by an external customer, of that organisation's premises and products.

Third Party   Audits carried out by personnel that are neither employees of the customer nor the supplier. They are usually employees of certification bodies or registrars such as BSI, TÜV and Yardley etc. These are also External Audits and are sometimes referred to as Certification Audits, Compliance Audits or Quality System Assessments.

2.3.1 First party (internal) audit

The type and content of any first party internal quality audit will vary according to the size and activities of the organisation. Its purpose is to:

- identify potential danger spots;
- eliminate wastage;
- verify that corrective action has been successfully achieved;
- provide a comparison between what the QMS or Quality Plan stipulates should be done and what is actually being done;
- confirm that everything is OK;
- identify non-compliance with previously issued instructions;
- identify deficiencies within the QMS;
- recommend any corrective actions that can be achieved to improve the system.

To meet these aims, the auditor must prepare an audit plan to determine whether the QMS is effectively achieving its stated quality objectives. It

Figure 2.1 First party (internal) audit

should be established as soon as possible and the procedures with which to carry out these audits should always be documented and available.

Note: To be effective, an internal audit should always include members of the organisation's quality control staff, provided that **they** are **not** responsible for the quality of that particular product.

The selection of the department to be audited should always be on a random basis and normally these internal audits will be completed every three months or so. Ideally, the audit should be pre-planned so that it covers all aspects of quality control within one calendar year.

Figure 2.2 Audit plan

The audit plan should:

- cover the specific areas and activities that are to be audited;
- stipulate the reasons why an internal audit is being completed (e.g. organisational changes, reported deficiencies, survey or routine check);
- stipulate the minimum qualifications of the personnel who are to conduct or assist with the audit;
- describe how the audit report should be finalised and submitted.

It is essential that management take timely corrective action on all deficiencies found during an internal audit. In some circumstances this can even mean going as far as having to review the statistical control methods that are used to indicate or predict the need for corrective action being carried out. Follow-up actions should include the verification of the implementation of corrective action, and the reporting of verification results.

2.3.2   External audit

All organisations are eventual 'suppliers' of their product or service and in order to stay in business they will have to provide proof that they can continue to provide a quality product/service. This is actually a 'measurement of their quality control' and usually takes the form of a supplier's evaluation, surveillance and/or external audit.

Figure 2.3 External audit

Note: Although the supplier may have been able to convince the purchaser that their QMS is effective, it is in the interests of the purchaser to conduct their own evaluation (i.e. audit) of the supplier. This is usually done on an irregular basis. The supplier must, of course, agree to the principle of purchaser evaluations being carried out and it is usual to find this as a separate clause in the contract.

External audits are audits carried out by an organisation independent of the organisation being audited, 'independence' being taken as there is no financial association other than by a contract. The audits are carried out by personnel that are neither employees of the customer nor the supplier and usually belong to certification bodies or registrars such as BSI, TÜV and Yardley, etc.

The purpose of both these audits is to ensure that:

- the organisation's QMS is being correctly and effectively implemented and that a corresponding compliance with the ISO 9001:2000 quality standard is maintained;
- any relevant legislation and standards are being adhered to;
- the system and procedures in operation are still effective and remain accurate for the working practices used;
- the data and information feedback from internal audits, complaints, compliments or routine work is considered at senior management level so that adjustments to the systems can be made;
- potential danger spots are identified, wastage eliminated and corrective action successfully achieved.

If the organisation is a manufacturer as opposed to being a service provider, then they will have to adhere to the relevant national and international quality management standards requiring manufacturers and suppliers to establish and maintain a fully documented method for the inspection of their system for quality control. Procedures for classifying lots, cataloguing characteristics, selecting samples and rules for acceptance and/or rejection criteria, together with procedures for segregating and screening rejected lots, need to be identified and developed.

Normally these audits are fairly simple, but (particularly when the material, product or service being purchased is complex) the purchaser will need to have a reasonably objective method of evaluating and measuring the efficiency of the quality control at the supplier's premises. The auditor needs to be certain that the system established by the supplier complies with laid down standards and is, above all, effective. This method is known as the 'supplier evaluation'.

2.3.2.1   Supplier evaluation

Part of the initial contract between a supplier (particularly those who actually manufacture a product) and a purchaser will normally stipulate that the supplier provides access, accommodation and facilities to the purchaser's inspectors. These facilities will depend upon the level of surveillance, but could require the supplier to provide:

- suitable office and administrative facilities;
- adequate work space for product verification;

Figure 2.4 Supplier evaluation

- access to those areas where work is in progress or to those which affect the work;
- help in documenting, inspecting and releasing products and services;
- the use of inspection and test devices and availability of personnel to operate them are necessary.

Evaluation team

The evaluation team will normally consist of a Lead Auditor assisted by two or more inspectors from the purchaser's organisation. These inspectors must be thoroughly skilled in the requirements of quality assurance and are normally drawn from the purchaser's own quality control section.

Pre-evaluation meeting

Before the evaluation team visits the supplier's premises, they must first be given the chance to:

- meet the supplier's staff to discuss the procedures being used;
- identify the areas that will be tested;

- decide which representative(s) of the supplier's organisation will be required to accompany the evaluation team during their inspection;
- agree dates and outline timetables, etc.

Study of the Quality Manual

Prior to commencing an evaluation, the Lead Auditor must be given a copy of the supplier's Quality Manual which he will scrutinise not only for its accuracy and clarity but also for its position compared to national and international standards and to see that it conforms to the relevant sections of ISO 9001:2000.

The evaluation

Having completed the pre-evaluation, the evaluation team will now go to the supplier's premises to fully scrutinise every aspect of the supplier's

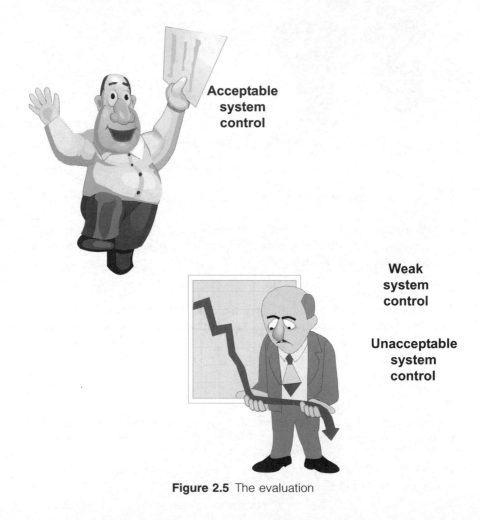

Figure 2.5 The evaluation

QMS. If the supplier is a manufacturer, then the evaluation team will pay particular attention to the supplier's design office, purchasing department, storekeeping, manufacturing, assembly and test facilities to see that the work carried out complies with the procedures and promises made in their Quality Manual.

During the evaluation, department heads will:

- first be required to describe to the team exactly how their quality control system works;
- provide examples of their quality control documentation;
- (possibly) be required to prove that certain sections have the correct documentation and that it is up to date.

In the case of manufacturers, they will:

- have to show how stock is received, accounted for and withdrawn from stores;
- show how the appropriate drawings are issued, updated and eventually disposed of;
- show how route cards and/or 'travellers' (that accompany partially completed work) are controlled;
- describe their sampling procedures to ascertain whether they conform to those laid down in the Quality Plan for that particular product;
- present evidence that their test equipment and other instruments have been regularly maintained and calibrated against a known source;
- show that rejected or unacceptable components and assemblies are clearly marked and segregated to avoid any chance of their accidental inclusion with other items that have already been accepted.

At the end of this evaluation, a meeting will be arranged between the evaluation team and the organisation's management to discuss their findings and ensure that there are not any misunderstandings, etc. The eventual evaluation report will then be formally presented at a meeting with the management and the result of this meeting could be one of the following.

Acceptable system control

This means that the evaluation has shown that the supplier has a satisfactory QMS, there are no deficiencies and the supplier has been able to give an assurance of quality. When this happens, there should be no reason why the purchaser should feel it necessary to demand any radical changes to the supplier's system.

Weak system control

This covers the situation where the evaluation team find several significant weaknesses in the supplier's system.

Note: If this happens, the supplier will have to take steps to overcome these failures and improve their QMS. Having done this, the supplier can then ask for another evaluation to be carried out to confirm that their quality now meets the required standards.

Unacceptable system control

This is when the evaluation team find that the number of deficiencies – or the lack of quality discipline at the supplier's premises – mean that the supplier will have to make radical changes to improve their overall QMS before they are anything like acceptable to the potential purchaser.

When the supplier has completed the necessary changes, they will then require a second evaluation to see that their improvements are satisfactory.

Note: Having been inspected, it is important that the records of this inspection are safely filed away in case they may be required to reinforce some point at a later stage or to provide statistical data for the analysis of a supplier's performance. This is sometimes referred to as vendor rating.

2.3.3   The surveillance or quality audit visit

Although an organisation may well have successfully passed their initial evaluation and the purchaser may well be satisfied that the supplier is capable of providing an assurance of quality, it cannot be assumed that the supplier will be able, or even capable of, retaining this status forever. Many things can happen to change this situation such as staff moving through promotion or natural wastage, changes in the product design that may be or have been necessary, or perhaps a new man-management philosophy.

For this reason it is quite possible that the purchaser might want to make irregular surveillance visits of the supplier's premises to further examine a particular aspect of their QMS. These surveillance or audit visits by the purchaser will be run on exactly the same lines as the supplier evaluation and are aimed at providing the purchaser with a confidence in the supplier and an assurance that they are still capable of providing the purchaser with the quality of service, goods and/or products that they require.

Note: The aim of these audit visits should be that all the important aspects of the quality control system are checked, in rotation.

2.3.3.1   Multiple evaluations and audits

It is possible that some suppliers might well be providing the same product to several different customers and it could just happen that all of these

Figure 2.6 The surveillance

customers ask to have an audit – at the same time. This obviously cannot be allowed to happen as the supplier would forever have people visiting the organisation and disturbing, not only the labour force, but also the production line. Purchasers can avoid this problem by agreeing to accept a secondary audit.

2.3.3.2 Secondary audit

If a purchaser indicates that they want to carry out an audit, the supplier can offer to provide the details of another customer's audit or the result of a third party's evaluation that has recently been carried out at their premises. If this does not quite cover the problem area sufficiently, then the supplier could offer to check in more detail the appropriate points raised by the purchaser.

2.4   Quality assurance during a product's or service's lifecycle

The life of a manufactured product or implemented service can be split into five stages as shown below:

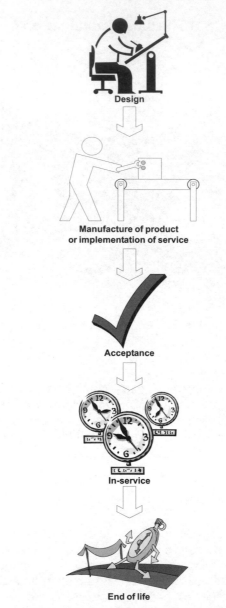

Design

Manufacture of product
or implementation of service

Acceptance

In-service

End of life

Figure 2.7 Quality assurance lifecycle

Figure 2.8 Quality assurance measurements

As quality assurance affects the product throughout its lifecycle, it is important that quality assurance procedures are introduced for design, manufacturing and acceptance stages, as well as in service utilisation.

2.4.1 Design stage

'*Quality must be designed into a product before manufacture or assembly*' (ISO 9004:2000).

Throughout the design stage of a service or product, the quality of that design must be regularly checked. Quality procedures have to be planned, written and implemented to predict and evaluate the fundamental and intrinsic reliability of the proposed design.

It doesn't matter whether the responsibility for the design of a product rests purely with the supplier, the purchaser, or is a joint function. It is essential that the designer is fully aware of the exact requirements of the project and has sound background knowledge of the relevant standards, information and procedures that will have to be adopted during the design stages.

This is extremely important, because the actions of the design office not only influence the maintenance of quality during manufacture and/or supply, but also play a major part in setting the quality level of the eventual product or service. From the point of view of a supplied product, if there is no quality control in a manufacturer's drawing office, then there is little chance of there ever being any on the shop floor. When the engineers are

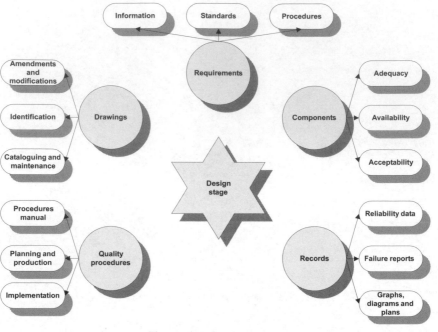

Figure 2.9 Design stage

trying to manufacture something (or a technician is attempting to assemble a system or module) to a set of drawings that have countless mistakes on them, what chance is there of them ever being able to produce an acceptable item!

These problems, although not specifically stipulated in ISO 9001:2000 should nevertheless be addressed. The design office (or team) should produce some sort of Procedures Manual, which lists and describes the routine QMS procedures and procedures that are required to turn a concept into a set of functional product or service drawings.

For all suppliers, these procedures will cover such activities as:

- the numbering of drawings and documents (i.e. document control);
- authorisation to issue amendments and modifications to documents and drawings;
- how to control changes to documents and drawings;
- the method of withdrawing obsolete documents and drawings;
- the identification, cataloguing and maintenance of documents and drawings.

For product manufacturers, in addition to these procedures, a manufacturer's design office will also:

- have to provide a complete listing of all the relevant components and their availability, acceptability and adequacy;
- be aware of all the advances in both materials and equipment that are currently available on today's market which are relevant to the product.
- assist in the analysis of failures, swiftly produce solutions and forestall costly work stoppages.

Note: One of the main problems to overcome is the ease with which the design office can make an arbitrary selection, but then find that the size and tolerance is completely inappropriate for the manufacturing or assembly process.

In order that the statistical significance of a particular failure can be assessed and correct retroactive action taken, it is essential that the design team also has access to all the records, failure reports and other data as soon as it is available.

The storage, maintenance and analysis of reliability data will require the design team to follow the progress of the product throughout its productive lifecycle, its many in-service and/or maintenance cycles and to take due note of customers' comments. The compilation and retention of this reliability data is not only very important, but also essential to the reliability of the product and/or service.

Nowadays, of course, most large design offices are computerised and use processors to store their records on discs so that these records can be continually updated and amended. This information (data) can then be used with standard software such as Computer Aided Design (CAD) programs and computer aided design facilities to produce lists, graphs and drawings. The possibilities are almost endless but there are associated problems such as security against virus attack and computer crashes.

2.4.2 Manufacturing stage

'*Manufacturing operations must be carried out under controlled conditions*' (ISO 9004:2000).

During all manufacturing processes (and throughout early in-service life), the product must be subjected to a variety of quality control procedures and checks in order to evaluate the degree of quality.

One of the first things that must be done is to predict the reliability of the product's design. This involves obtaining sufficient statistical data so as to be able to estimate the actual reliability of the design before a product is manufactured.

All the appropriate engineering data has to be carefully examined, particularly the reliability ratings of recommended parts and components.

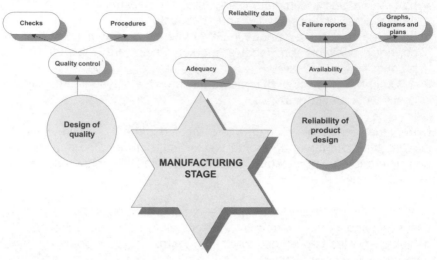

Figure 2.10 Manufacturing stage

The designer then extrapolates and interpolates this data and uses probability methods to examine the reliability of a proposed design.

Note: Design deficiencies such as assembly errors, operator learning, motivational or fatigue factors, latent defects and improper part selection are frequently uncovered during this process.

2.4.3   Acceptance stage

'*The quality of a product must be proved before being accepted*' (ISO 9004:2000).

During the acceptance stage, the product or service will be subjected to a series of tests designed to confirm that the workmanship of the product/service fully meets the levels of quality required, or stipulated by the user and that the product/service performs the required function correctly.

In the case of a manufactured product, it will range from environmental tests of individual components to field testing complete systems. Three mathematical expressions are commonly used to measure reliability and each of these expressions can be applied to a part, component assembly or an entire system. They are, probability function (PF), failure rate (FR) and mean time between failures (MTBF).

2.4.4   In-service stage

'*Evaluation of product performance during typical operating conditions and feedback of information gained through field use – improves product capability*' (ISO 9004:2000).

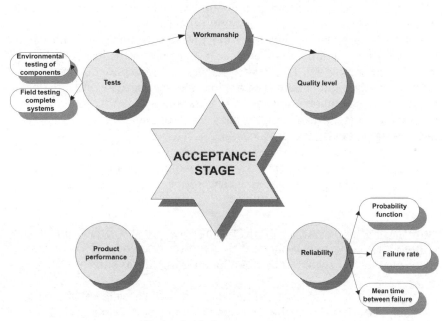

Figure 2.11 Acceptance stage

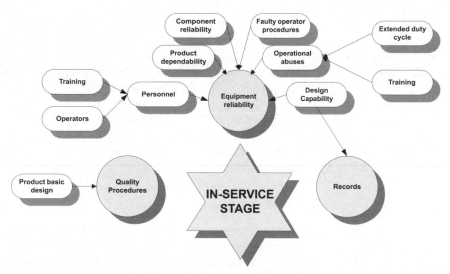

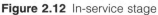

Figure 2.12 In-service stage

During the in-service stage the purchaser is, of course, principally concerned with system and equipment reliability.

Although reliability is based on the product system's generic design (and can be easily proved by statistics) its practical reliability is often far less design dependent. This difference can be due to poor documentation, faulty operating procedures, operating the system beyond its design capability or operational abuses (e.g. personal – extended duty cycles – neglected maintenance – training etc.). Each of these hazards will have a detrimental effect on the product/service.

For manufactured products, the problems associated with poorly trained, poorly supported, or poorly motivated maintenance personnel with respect to reliability and dependability require careful assessment and quantification.

Note: According to recent studies completed by the British Institute of Management, the maintenance technician (or engineer) still remains the primary cause of reliability degradations during the in-service stage.

The most important factor that affects the overall reliability of a modern product, nevertheless, is the increased number of individual components that are required in that product. Since most system failures are actually caused by the failure of a single component, the reliability of each individual component must be considerably better than the overall system reliability.

Information obtained from in-service use and field failures are enormously useful (always assuming that they are entirely accurate, of course!) in evaluating a product's performance during typical operating conditions. But the main reason for accumulating failure reports from the field is to try to improve the product. This can be achieved by analysing the reports, finding out what caused the failure and taking steps to prevent it from recurring in the future.

Because of this requirement, quality standards for the maintenance, repair and inspection of in-service products have had to be laid down in engineering standards, handbooks and local operating manuals (written for specific items and equipment). These publications are used by maintenance engineers and should always include the most recent amendments. It is **essential** that quality assurance personnel also use the same procedures for their inspections.

2.4.5   Supplier's responsibilities

The supplier's prime responsibility must always be to ensure that anything **and everything** leaving their organisation whether it is a document, product or service conforms to the specific requirements of the purchaser – particularly with regard to quality.

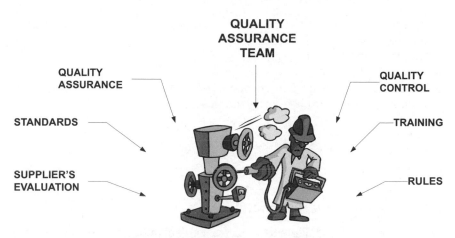

Figure 2.13 Supplier's responsibilities

In this respect, the supplier is responsible for ensuring that:

- all managerial staff, from the most junior to the most senior, firmly believe in the importance of quality control and quality assurance and understand how to implement them;
- managerial staff create an atmosphere in which quality assurance rules are obeyed and not simply avoided just because they are inconvenient, time consuming, laborious or just too boring to bother with;
- there is an accepted training scheme to ensure that all members of the firm are regularly brought up to date with the ongoing and the latest requirements of quality assurance;
- there is a quality assurance team available to oversee and make sure that quality control and quality assurance are carried out at all times and **at all levels**, within their premises.

Lack of quality control and quality assurance can cause a supplier providing manufactured products to:

- replace scrapped material or have to rework unsatisfactory material;
- reinspect and reprocess material returned as unsatisfactory by the purchaser;
- lose money by having to send staff to the purchaser's premises to sort out their complaints of unsatisfactory labour;
- lose money through a major quality failure halting production;
- lose money through field repairs, replacements and other work having to be carried out under warranty;
- lose money by having to carry out investigations into claims of unsatisfactory work;

- lose money by having to investigate alternative methods of producing an article without quality failures;
- lose their image or reputation;
- lose market potential;
- have to acknowledge complaints, claims, liabilities and be subject to waste of human and financial resources;

But most of all...

- lose customers!

2.4.6   Purchaser's responsibilities

Quite a number of problems associated with service or product quality are usually the fault of the purchaser! Obviously, the purchaser can only expect to get what he ordered. It is, therefore, extremely important that the actual order is not only correct, but also provides the supplier or manufacturer with all the relevant (and accurate) information required completing the task.

   In the case of a manufactured product, this can be achieved by providing a drawing, which contains all the relevant details such as:

- type of material to be used;
- the materials grade or condition;
- the specifications that are to be followed;
- all the relevant dimensional data, sizes, tolerances etc.
- reference to one of the accepted standards.

Note: Where possible, the graphic order/drawing should be to scale.

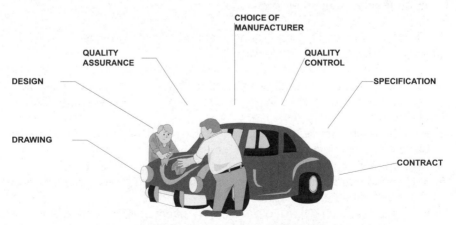

Figure 2.14 Purchaser's responsibilities

In the case of a service provider, the supplier must have the service specification fully defined, documented and agreed before work is commenced.

By not insisting that the supplier abides by a set of recognised quality standards, the purchaser can be involved in:

- delays in being able to use the product or service and the possibility of the purchaser losing orders because of it;
- possible increases in their organisation, operation, maintenance down-time and repair costs;
- dissatisfaction with goods and services;
- health and safety aspects (now a mandatory requirement of ISO 9001:2000);
- lack of confidence in the supplier.

2.5 The effect of ISO 9001:2000's new requirements

In addition to the requirements replicated from the previous 20-element ISO 9001:1994 standard auditors will, in future, now have to address the following.

2.5.1 Customer focus

Organisations will have to have in place a system for determining customer needs and expectations including:

- requirements not specified by the customer but necessary for intended service or product use;
- obligations related to the product and/or service, as well as regulatory and legal requirements;
- a system for monitoring customer satisfaction and/or dissatisfaction;
- a system for ensuring that customer needs and expectations are determined, converted into requirements, and fulfilled with the overall aim of achieving customer satisfaction.

2.5.2 Customer communication

The organisation will need to have in place a process for customer communications relating to: inquiries, order handling, or contracts (including amendments); customer feedback (including complaints). A process also needs to be established by the organisation for monitoring customer satisfaction and/or dissatisfaction as one of the measurements of quality management system performance.

2.5.3   Training

In the future, evidence that training has been provided will not be enough. An evaluation of the **effectiveness** of training will also be required. Another requirement for top management is that the requirements and adherence to the organisation's QMS processes and of process effectiveness shall be effectively communicated among all tiers and functions of the organisation.

2.5.4   Legal and regulatory compliance

Increased emphasis has now been placed on the role of top management to develop and improve the system, integrate legal and regulatory requirements, and establish measurable objectives at appropriate levels of the organisation.

2.5.5   QMS development and improvement

To satisfy the requirements of ISO 9001:2000, top management must now provide evidence of its commitment to the development and improvement of their QMS. This evidence must include a procedure that lays emphasis on the importance of meeting customer needs, as well as regulatory and legal requirements.

The organisation will also need to show how it plans and manages the processes necessary for the continuous improvement of the quality management system through the use of the quality policies, objectives, audit results, data analyses, corrective and preventive actions, and management review.

2.5.6   Product conformity

From a manufacturer's point of view, the requirement for an organisation to identify, provide and maintain the facilities it needs to achieve conformity of product (including: workspace and associated facilities; equipment, hardware and software; and supporting services) has now been expanded to include the identification and management of the work environment and, in particular, the need to consider the human and physical factors required to achieve conformity of product.

2.5.7   Measurement and continual improvement

Measurement and monitoring activities are a new requirement. Organisations must determine the requirements and uses of 'applicable methodologies,' including statistical techniques.

To achieve this requirement, the organisation must establish a process for collecting and analysing appropriate data to determine the suitability and effectiveness of the quality management system, to identify potential improvements and data to provide information on customer satisfaction and/or dissatisfaction and conformance to customer requirements.

2.5.8 Quality Management System requirements

'A Quality Management System is a system to establish a quality policy and quality objectives and to achieve these objectives' (ISO 9000:2000).

It is an organisational structure of responsibilities, activities, resources and events that together provide procedures and methods of implementation to ensure the capability of an organisation to meet quality requirements.

Within ISO 9001:2000, there is now greater emphasis on the structure of a process-orientated QMS. **Note:** The following section (which was part of a previous publication by the author) is included here as a reminder for auditors.

2.6 Basic requirements of a Quality Management System

To be successful, an organisation must:

● be able to offer products and/or services that satisfy a customer's expectations;
● agree with the relevant standards and specifications of a contract;
● be available at competitive prices;

and

● supply at a cost that will still bring a profit to that organisation.

They must, above all, provide a quality product and/or service that will promote further procurement and recommendations and they must be able to prove to their potential purchasers that they are capable of continually providing a quality product/service. To satisfy these requirements an organisation's QMS has to encompass all the different levels of quality control that are required during the various stages of design, manufacture, supply, incorporation/installation and acceptance of a product and/or service and be capable of guaranteeing quality acceptance.

These requirements are covered by national, European and international standards. However, although these standards may vary slightly

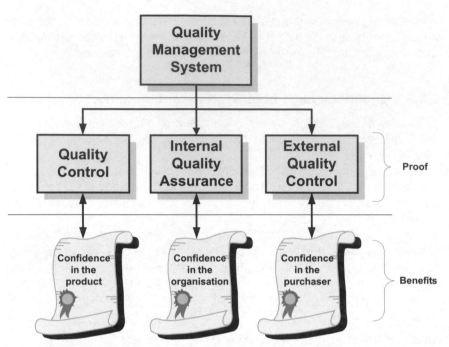

Figure 2.15 Quality Management System – organisational structure

from country to country, they are very similar and cover the following topics:

- organisational structure;
- measurement of quality assurance;
- the contract;
- design control;
- purchasing and procurement;
- production control;
- product testing;
- handling, storage, packaging and delivery;
- after-sales service.

2.6.1   Quality Management System principles

The first thing that ISO 9001:2000 requires is for an organisation to set up and fully document their position with regard to quality assurance. These documents comprise the organisation's QMS and describe the organisation's capability for supplying goods and services that will comply with laid down quality standards. It contains a general description of the organisa-

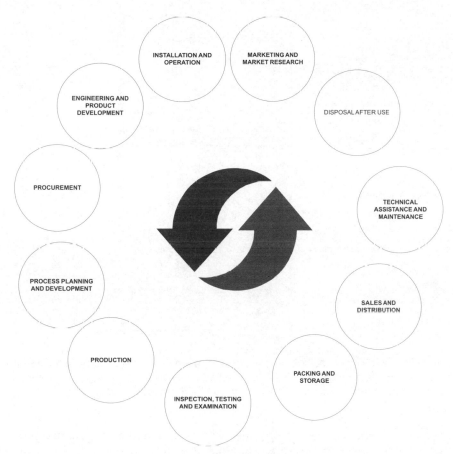

Figure 2.16 Quality loop

tion's attitude to quality assurance and specific details about the quality assurance and quality control within that organisation.

To be successful an organisation must be able to prove that they are capable of producing the component, product or service to the customer's complete satisfaction so that it conforms exactly to the purchaser's specific requirements and that it is always of the desired quality. An organisation's QMS is, therefore, the organisational structure of responsibilities, procedures, processes and resources for carrying out quality management and as such must be planned and developed in order to be capable of maintaining a consistent level of quality control.

The QMS must be structured to the organisation's own particular type of business and should consider all functions such as customer liaison, designing, purchasing, subcontracting, manufacturing, training, installation, updating of quality control techniques and the accumulation of quality

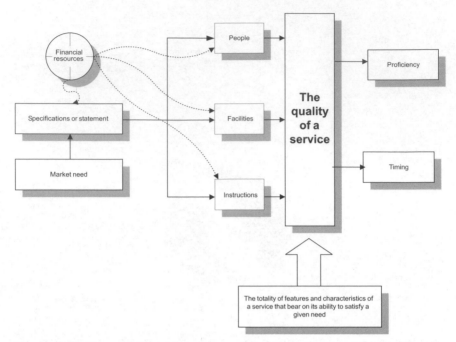

Figure 2.17 Some of the determinants and measurements of the quality of a service. (This is an extract from BS 4778:1979 which has been reproduced with the kind permission of BSI. The 1979 edition has been superseded but these figures are included here since they illustrate the concept.)

records. In most organisations this sort of information will normally be found in the organisation's Quality Manual.

The type of QMS chosen will, of course, vary from organisation to organisation depending upon its size and capability. There are no set rules as to exactly how these documents should be written. However, they should – as a minimum requirement – be capable of showing the potential customer exactly how the manufacturer or supplier is equipped to achieve and maintain the highest level of quality throughout the various stages of design, production, installation and servicing.

As an example, some of the determinants and measures of the quality of a service are shown in Figure 2.17 whilst those affecting the quality of a product are shown in Figure 2.18.

2.6.2   Quality Management System approach

Customers require products and/or services that continually meet their needs and expectations and in order to be profitable, an organisation must be able to offer them so that it can continually achieve customer satisfaction and satisfy its customers' requirements. As well as providing a

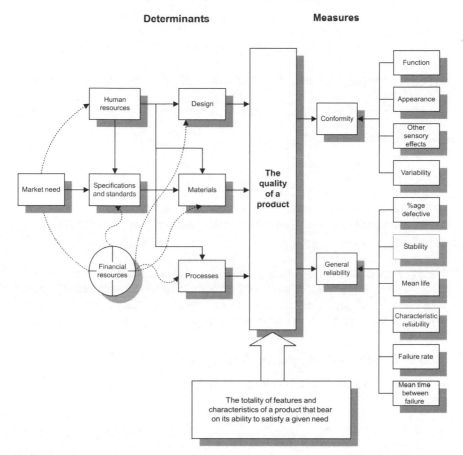

Figure 2.18 Some of the determinants and measurements of the quality of a product. (This is an extract from BS 4778:1979 which has been reproduced with the kind permission of BSI. The 1979 edition has been superseded but these figures are included here since they illustrate the concept.)

framework for providing customer satisfaction, a QMS also provides confidence (to the organisation and to its customers) that the organisation is capable of providing products and services that consistently fulfil requirements. This is achieved by:

- determining the needs and expectations of the customer;
- establishing the quality policy and quality objectives of the organisation;
- determining the processes and responsibilities necessary to attain the quality objectives;
- establishing measures for the effectiveness of each process towards attaining the quality objectives;

- applying the measures to determine the current effectiveness of each process;
- determining means of preventing non-conformities and eliminating their causes;
- looking for opportunities to improve the effectiveness and efficiency of processes;
- determining and prioritising those improvements which can provide optimum results;
- planning the strategies, processes and resources to deliver the identified improvements;
- implementing the plan;
- monitoring the effects of the improvements;
- assessing the results against the expected outcomes;
- reviewing the improvement activities to determine appropriate follow-up actions.

Note: Any organisation that adopts the above approach will create confidence in the capability of its processes and the reliability of its products. It will also provide a basis for continual improvement and can lead to increased customer satisfaction.

2.6.3   Quality Management System reliability

For an organisation to derive any real benefit from a QMS, everyone in the organisation must:

- fully appreciate that quality assurance is absolutely essential to their future;
- know how they can assist in achieving quality;
- be stimulated and encouraged so to do.

In addition, their organisation's QMS must be fully documented and it must be capable of providing an adequate and uninterrupted control over all internal and external activities that affect the quality of a service or product. This QMS must emphasise all preventive actions that are required to avoid problems recurring and working systems will have to be developed, issued and maintained.

These regulations and requirements will normally be found in the organisation's Quality Manual.

2.6.4   Quality Management System structure

An organisation's QMS defines the policy, organisation, and responsibilities for the management of quality within that organisation. It ensures that all activities comply with an agreed set of rules, regulations and guidelines

QMS – Quality Model

Figure 2.19 ISO 9001:2000 Quality Model

Table 2.1 QMS documentation

Level 1	Quality Manual	The main policy document that establishes the QMS and how it meets the requirements of ISO 9001:2000.
Level 2	Processes	The Core Business Process plus Supporting Processes that describe the activities required to implement the QMS and to meet the policy requirements made in the Quality Manual.
Level 3	Quality Procedures	A description of the method by which quality system activities are managed.
Level 4	Work Instructions	A description of how a specific task is carried out.

and that the end product (i.e. the deliverable) conforms to the customer's (i.e. the user's) contractual requirements.

A QMS can only be effective if it is fully documented, understood and followed by all. Within the ISO 9001:2000 Quality Model, there are four levels of documentation, and these are structured as shown in Fig. 2.19.

2.6.4.1 Quality Manual

This is the main policy document that establishes the QMS and how it meets the requirements of ISO 9001:2000. It provides general information on the system (i.e. objectives, goals, roles, organisation and responsibilities).

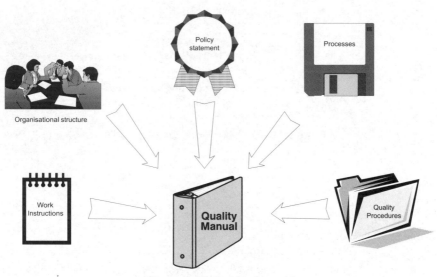

Figure 2.20 Quality Manual

An organisation's Quality Manual is the formal record of that firm's QMS. It:

- is a rule book by which an organisation functions;
- is a source of information from which the client may derive confidence;
- provides consistent information, both internally and externally, about the organisation's QMS;
- is a means of defining the responsibilities and interrelated activities of every member of the organisation;

- is a vehicle for auditing, reviewing and evaluating the organisation's QMS.

To be effective:

- the Quality Manual will have to include a firm statement of the organisation's policy towards quality control;
- it must contain details of their quality assurance section, its structure and organisation, together with a description of their responsibilities;
- it must indicate quality assurance training programmes etc.

The Quality Manual will describe how the organisation:

- documents and records inspections;
- how their goods inwards facility operates;
- how they monitor quality.

Note: When complex assemblies or multi-part contracts are required, separate instructions may have to be included in the Quality Manual in order to cover individual parts of the contract. These types of instructions are called Quality Plans.

The Quality Manual will also identify the organisation's business-critical processes and their associated Quality Procedures (QPs) and Work Instructions (WIs). The Quality Manual will also provide examples of the various forms and documentation used by the manufacturer – such as production control forms, inspection sheets and documents used to purchase components from subcontractors.

Note: For a complete description and guidance on how to develop a Quality Manual, the reader is referred to ISO 10013.

2.6.4.2 Processes

Processes describe the activities required to implement the QMS and to meet the policy requirements made in the Quality Manual. Core Business Processes describe the end-to-end activities involved in project management and are supplemented by a number of supporting processes.

2.6.4.3 Quality Procedures

QPs are formal documents that describe the method by which the Core Business and supporting processes are managed.
    They describe how the policy objectives of the Quality Manual can be met in practice and how these processes are controlled. They contain the basic documentation used for planning and controlling all activities that impact on quality.

2.6.4.4   Work Instructions

WIs describe in detail how individual tasks and activities are to be carried out, e.g. what is to be done, by whom and when it has to be completed.

2.6.5   Quality Plan

The accepted definition (as provided in ISO 9000:2000) of a Quality Plan is that it is '*a document specifying the QMS elements and the resources to be applied in a specific case*'. In setting out the specific quality practices, resources and sequence of activities relevant to a particular product, project or contract, a Quality Plan, therefore, ensures that specific requirements for quality are appropriately planned and addressed. It should state its purpose, to what it applies its quality objectives (in measurable terms), specific exclusions and, of course, its period of validity.

Quality Plans describe how the QMS is applied to a specific product or contract. They may be used to demonstrate how the quality requirements

Figure 2.21 Quality Plan

of a particular contract will be met, and to monitor and assess adherence to those requirements. While a Quality Plan usually refers to the appropriate parts of the Quality Manual, it can be used in conjunction with a QMS or as a stand-alone document.

Note: Quality Plans provide a collated summary of the requirements for a specific activity. They include less information than the organisation's QMS but, with all the detail brought together, the requirement for performance should be more readily understandable and the risk of non-conformance and misinterpretation of intentions should be reduced.

Quality assurance for the manufacture of complex assemblies can be very difficult to stipulate in a contract especially if the most important inspections have to be left until the assembly is almost complete – and by which time many of the subassemblies and components will have become almost inaccessible! In these cases it is essential for the organisation's Quality Manager to develop and produce a Quality Plan that details all the important information that has to be provided to the shop floor management.

The Quality Plan will cover all of the quality practices and resources that are going to be used, the sequence of events relevant to that product, the specific allocation of responsibilities, methods, QPs and WIs, together with the details of the testing, inspection, examination and audit programme stages. The Quality Plan should, nevertheless, be flexible and written in such a way that it is possible to modify its content to reflect changing circumstances.

The main requirement of a Quality Plan, however, is to provide the customer (and the workforce) with clear, concise instructions and guidance as well as the appropriate inspection methods and procedures; the results of inspections (including rejections) and details of any concessions issued for rework or repair. All these must be clearly recorded and available for a purchaser's future (possible) examination.

A well-thought-out Quality Plan will divide the project, service, product or assembly work into stages, show what type of inspection has to be completed at the beginning, during, or end of each stage and indicate how these details should be recorded on the final document. The Quality Plan should be planned and developed in conjunction with design, development, manufacturing, subcontract and installation work and ensure that all functions have been fully catered for.

One of the main objectives of quality planning is to identify any special or unusual requirements, processes, techniques including those requirements that are unusual by reason of newness, unfamiliarity, lack of experience and/or absence of precedents. As ISO 9004:2000 points out, if the contract specifies that Quality Plans are required, then these Quality Plans should fully cover the following areas and ensure that:

- design, contract, development, manufacturing and installation activities are well documented and adequate;
- all controls, processes, inspection equipment, fixtures, tooling, manpower resources and skills that an organisation must have to achieve the required quality, have been identified, recorded and the necessary action taken to obtain any additional components, documentation etc. that is required;
- quality control, inspection and testing techniques (including the development of new instrumentation) have been updated;
- any new measurement technique (or any measurement involving a measurement capability that exceeds the known state of the art) that is required to inspect the product, has been identified and action taken to develop that capability;
- standards of acceptability for all features and requirements (including those which contain a subjective element) have been clearly recorded;
- compatibility of design, manufacturing process, installation, inspection procedures and applicable documentation have been assured well before production begins;
- as each special requirement is identified, the means for testing and being able to prove successfully that the product or service is capable of successfully complying with the requirements has be considered.

Note: In certain cases (e.g. new techniques), existing inspection practices may be inadequate and new ones will have to be developed.

The integration of special or unusual requirements into the QMS must be carefully investigated, planned and documented.

A Quality Plan is effectively a subset of the actual Quality Manual. The layout of the Quality Plan is very similar to that of the Quality Manual and refers (other than system-specific QPs and WIs) normally to the QPs and Work Instructions contained in that Quality Manual.

The following briefly describes how each of the main requirements of ISO 9001:2000 is covered in a Quality Plan.

2.6.5.1 Management responsibility

The Quality Plan should show who is responsible for:

- ensuring activities are planned, implemented, controlled and monitored;
- communicating requirements and resolving problems;
- reviewing audit results;
- authorising exemption requests;
- implementing corrective action requests.

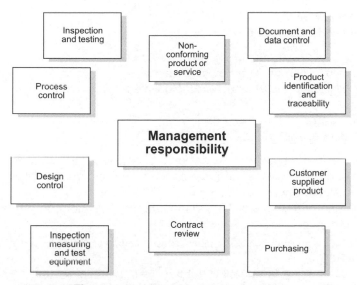

Figure 2.22 Management responsibility

Where the necessary documentation already exists under the present QMS, the Quality Plan need only refer to a specific situation or specification.

Document and data control
Document and data control should refer to:

- what is provided and how it is controlled;
- how related documents will be identified;
- how and by whom access to the documents can be obtained;
- how and by whom the original documents are reviewed and approved.

Process control
Process control may include:

- the procedures/instructions;
- process steps;
- methods to monitor and control processes;
- service/product characteristics.

The plan could also include details of:

- reference criteria for workmanship;
- special and qualified processes;
- tools, techniques and methods to be used.

Contract review

Contract review should cover:

- when, how and by whom the review is made;
- how the results are to be documented;
- how conflicting instructions or ambiguities are resolved.

Design control

Design control should indicate:

- when, how and by whom the design process, validation and verification of the design output is carried out, controlled and documented;
- any customer involvement;
- applicable codes of practice, standards, specifications and regulatory requirements.

Purchasing

Under the heading of purchasing the following should be indicated:

- the important products to be purchased;
- the source and requirements relating to them;
- the method, evaluation, selection and control of subcontractors;
- the need for a subcontractor's Quality Plan in order to satisfy the regulatory requirements applicable to purchase products/services.

Customer supplied product

Customer supplied products should refer to:

- how they are identified and controlled;
- how they are verified as meeting specified requirements;
- how non-conformance is dealt with.

Product identification and traceability

If traceability is a requirement then the plan should:

- define its scope and extent (including how services/products are identified);
- indicate how contractual and regulatory authority traceability requirements are identified and incorporated into working documents;
- indicate how records are to be generated, controlled and distributed.

Inspection and testing

Inspection and testing should indicate:

- any inspection and test plan;
- how the subcontractor's product shall be verified;
- the location of inspection and test points;
- procedures and acceptance criteria;

- witness verification points (customers as well as regulatory);
- where, when and how the customer requires third parties to perform:
  - type tests;
  - witness testing;
  - service/product verification;
  - material, service/product, process or personnel certification.

Inspection, measuring and test equipment

Inspection, measuring and test equipment should:

- refer to the identity of the equipment;
- refer to the method of calibration;
- indicate and record calibration status and usage of the equipment;
- indicate specific requirements for the identification of inspection and test status.

Non-conforming service/product

Under the heading of nonconforming service/product, an indication should be given:

- of how such a service/product is identified and segregated;
- the degree or type of rework allowed;
- the circumstances under which the supplier can request concessions.

Details should also be provided with respect to:

- corrective and preventive action;
- handling, storage, packaging, preservation and delivery.

Other considerations

Quality Plans should:

- indicate key quality records (i.e. what they are, how long they should be kept, where and by whom.
- suggest how legal or regulatory requirements are to be satisfied;
- specify the form in which records should be kept (e.g. paper, microfilm or disc);
- define liability, storage, retrievability, disposition and confidentiality requirements;
- include the nature and extent of quality audits to be undertaken;
- indicate how the audit results are to used to correct and prevent recurrence of deficiencies;
- show how the training of staff in new or revised operating methods is to be completed.

Where servicing is a specified requirement, suppliers should state their intentions to assure conformance to applicable servicing requirements, such as:

- regulatory and legislative requirements;
- industry codes and practices;
- service level agreements;
- training of customer personnel;
- availability of initial and ongoing support during the agreed time period;
- statistical techniques, where relevant.

Note: Work is now well under way with a new standard (ISO 10005) which will provide the reader with guidance on how to produce Quality Plans as well as including helpful suggestions on how to maintain an organisation's quality activities.

2.6.6   Quality records

Quality records provide objective evidence of activities performed or results achieved.

Records of QMS inspections and tests concerning the design, testing, survey, audit and review of a product or service are the evidence that a supplier is capable of and is indeed meeting the quality requirements of the customer.

Records such as QMS audit reports, calibration of test and measuring equipment, inspections, tests, approvals, concessions, etc., ensure that an organisation is capable of proving the effectiveness of their QMS.

Records, therefore, are important parts of quality management and the QMS will have to identify exactly what type of record is to be made, at what stage of the production process they should be made and who should make them etc. To be of any real value it is essential that these records are covered by clear, concise instructions and procedures. Above all, the

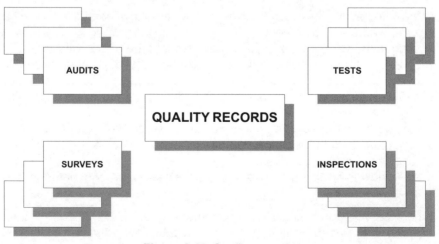

Figure 2.23 Quality records

storage of records should be systematic and capable of being easily and quickly accessed.

Having agreed and decided on the necessity for records, the next step is to:

- establish methods for making changes, modifications, revisions and additions to these records;
- establish methods for accounting for the documents;
- show their retention time;
- lay down methods for the disposal of those that are superseded or become out of date;
- show how they should be stored.

These procedures would be written up as QPs and will normally form part of the Quality Manual. WIs should also be available to show how important it is to keep records of defects, diagnosis of their causes and details of the corrective action that was carried out together with the success or failure of this corrective action.

If this information is stored in a computer, then it is essential that the integrity of that system **must** also be satisfactorily assured.

The retention of records is an aspect that is far too often overlooked by organisations. Records are very important, not only from a historical point of view, but also as a means to settling disputes about bad workmanship, identifying faults and settling production problems whether this be internally, by the supplier, or externally, by the organisation.

2.7 Quality organisational structure

2.7.1 Management

The main requirement of the organisation's management is that they establish, define and document their organisation's policy, objectives and commitments to quality. This document must include details of the organisation's Quality Management System (QMS) and the aims, policies, organisation and procedures that are essential to demonstrate that they agree with the requirements of ISO 9001:2000.

Having established their overall position, the management will then have to:

- develop, control, co-ordinate, supervise and monitor their corporate quality policy and ensure that this policy is understood and maintained throughout the organisation;
- ensure that the organisation's QMS always meets the requirements of the national, European or international standard that that particular organisation has chosen to work to and where this fails to happen, see that corrective actions are carried out;
- define objectives such as fitness for use;

Figure 2.24 Quality organisational requirements

- ensure that the performance, safety and reliability of a product or service is correct and make sure that the costs associated with these objectives are kept to a reasonable figure.

Note: Organisations having difficulty in establishing their own particular level of managerial responsibility with regard to organisation quality assurance should obtain a copies of BS 6143:1992 'Guide to the economics of quality' Parts 1 and 2. These standards are available from the BSI and are a user-friendly guide to:

  - the costs for continuous improvement and Total Quality Management (TQM) (Part 1);
  - the costs of defect prevention and a study of the various activities and losses due to internal or external failures (Part 2).

2.7.2   The Quality Manager

Quality assurance is concerned with a consistency of quality and an agreed level of quality. To achieve these aims the organisation must be firmly committed to the fundamental principle of consistently supplying the right quality product. Equally, a purchaser must be committed to the fundamental principle of only accepting the right quality product.

Thus, a commitment within all levels of an organisation (manufacturer, supplier or purchaser) to the basic principles of quality assurance and quality control is required. It is, therefore, essential that the management representative, who is completely independent of all other responsibilities, deals solely with quality matters. This person is called the 'Quality Manager'.

The Quality Manager will answer directly to the Managing Director and will be responsible for all matters regarding the quality of the end product together with the activities of **all** sections within the organisation's premises.

In small organisations this requirement might even be part of the General Manager's duties, but regardless of who it may be, it is essential that this person must be someone who is completely independent of any manufacturing or user function and has a thorough working knowledge of the requirements and recommendations of ISO 9001:2000.

In addition, owing to the importance of quality assurance, it is essential that the Quality Manager is fully qualified (both technically and administratively) and can quickly exert (show) his position and authority.

The Quality Manager's job is usually a very busy one (even in a small organisation!), and the Quality Manager's responsibilities are spread over a wide area which covers all of the organisation's operations.

Who controls Quality in a company?

Management
?

The
Quality
Manager
?

All of them!

The
staff
?

Figure 2.25 Who controls quality?

2.7.2.1   General functional description

The Quality Manager is responsible for ensuring that the organisation's QMS is defined, implemented, audited and monitored in order to ensure that the organisation's deliverables comply with both the customer's quality and safety standards together with the requirements of ISO 9001:2000.

2.7.2.2   Tasks

The Quality Manager reports directly to the general manager and his tasks will include:

- ensuring the consistency of the organisation QMS;
- ensuring compliance of the organisation QMS with ISO 9001:2000;
- maintenance and effectiveness of the organisation QMS;
- ensuring that the quality message is transmitted to and understood by everyone.

2.7.2.3   Responsibilities

- The Quality Manager is responsible for:
- ensuring that the Quality Manual and individual Quality Plans are kept up to date;
- assisting and advising with the preparation of organisation procedures;
- producing, reviewing and updating the organisation QMS;
- ensuring compliance with the organisation QMS by means of frequent audits;
- maintaining organisation quality records;
- producing, auditing and maintaining division, section and project Quality Plans;
- identifying potential/current problem areas within the organisation's lifecycle through analysis of organisation error reports;
- holding regular division quality audits.

2.7.2.4   Co-ordination

The Quality Manager shall:

- act as the focal point for all organisation quality matters within the organisation;
- co-ordinate and verify all internal procedures and instructions are in accordance with the recommendations of ISO 9001:2000;
- operate the QMS as described in the Quality Manual and ensure that its regulations are observed.

Above all the Quality Manager must always ensure that the customer's interests are protected. Even if this means, at times, that he and his division become very unpopular with the rest of the organisation and sometimes they even have to assume the mantel of organisation 'scapegoat'!

3

ISO 9001:2000 CHECKLISTS

There now follows a number of sections that have been constructed with the specific aim of assisting auditors to complete internal and external audits. They consist of:

3.1	**ISO 9001:2000 headings**	A complete list of the sections and subsections making up ISO 9001:2000 requirements.
3.2	**Comparison between ISO 9001:2000 and ISO 9001:1994**	A complete list of the sections and subsections making up ISO 9001:2000 requirements cross-referenced to the previous ISO 9001:1994 elements.
3.3	**Counter-comparison between ISO 9001:1994 and ISO 9001:2000**	A complete list of the elements making up ISO 9001:1994 cross-referenced to the sections and subsections of ISO 9001:2000.
3.4	**Comparison of ISO 9001:2000 headings between CD2, FDIS and the IS**	A historical overview of the changes made to the basic structure of ISO 9001:2000 sections and subsections during the review process.
3.5	**Complete index for ISO 9001:2000**	A listing of all the main topics and subjects covered in ISO 9001:2000.
3.6	**ISO 9001:2000 crosscheck to a 1994 QMS**	A form that can be used to list an organisation's 1994 QMS, its business processes, quality procedures, work instructions and their correspondence to ISO 9001:2000.

3.7	**ISO 9001:2000 – explanation and likely documentation**	A brief explanation of the specific requirements (i.e. the 'shalls') of each element of ISO 9001:2000 together with a description of the likely documentation that an organisation would need to have in place to meet the requirements.
3.8	**Audit check sheet**	A list of the most important questions an auditor should ask.
3.9	**Stage audit check sheet**	List of the most important questions that an external auditor is likely to ask when evaluating an organisation for the:

- design stage;
- manufacturing stage;
- acceptance stage;
- in-service stage.

3.10	**Additional (general purpose) audit checks**	Lists of the most important questions that an external auditor would have used to evaluate a previous ISO 9001:1994 QMS.
3.11	**A selection of audit forms**	A selection of forms used by auditors.
3.12	**ISO 9001:2000 – elements covered and outstanding**	A checklist used by auditors to confirm that the client's QMS fully covers the requirements (i.e. elements) of ISO 9001:2000.
3.13	**Acronyms and abbreviations used in Quality**	
3.14	**Glossary of terms used in Quality**	

Note: A copy of these checklists is available on CD-ROM for a small fee from the author in Rich Text format or Word 95-2000. He can be contacted via stingray@herne.org.uk if you would like to take advantage of this service.

3.1 ISO 9001:2000 headings

1   Scope
1.1   General
1.2   Application

2   Normative reference

3   Terms and definitions

4   Quality Management System
4.1   General requirements
4.2   Documentation requirements
4.2.1 General
4.2.2 Quality Manual
4.2.3 Control of documents
4.2.4 Control of records

5   Management responsibility
5.1   Management commitment
5.2   Customer focus
5.3   Quality policy
5.3   Planning
5.3.1 Quality objectives
5.3.2 Quality Management System planning
5.5   Responsibility, authority and communication
5.5.1 Responsibility and authority
5.5.1 Management representative
5.5.2 Internal communication
5.6   Management review
5.6.1 General
5.6.2 Review input
5.6.3 Review output

6   Resource management
6.1   Provision of resources
6.2   Human resources
6.2.1 General
6.2.2 Competence, awareness and training
6.3   Infrastructure
6.4   Work environment

7   Product realisation
7.1   Planning of product realisation
7.2   Customer-related processes

3.2 Comparison between ISO 9001:2000 and ISO 9001:1994

Clause No.	ISO 9001:2000 title	ISO 9001:1994 correspondence
1	Scope	1
1.1	General	
1.2	Application	
2	Normative reference	2
3	Terms and definitions	3
4	Quality Management System (title only)	
4.1	General requirements	4.2.1
4.2	Documentation requirements (title only)	
4.2.1	General	4.2.2
4.2.2	Quality Manual	4.2.1
4.2.3	Control of documents	4.5.1, 4.5.2, 4.5.3
4.2.4	Control of records	4.16
5	Management responsibility (title only)	
5.1	Management commitment	4.1.1
5.2	Customer focus	4.3.2
5.3	Quality policy	4.1.1
5.4	Planning (title only)	
5.4.1	Quality objectives	4.1.1

Comparison between ISO 9001:2000 and ISO 9001:1994 *Continued*

Clause No.	ISO 9001:2000 title	ISO 9001:1994 correspondence
5.4.2	Quality Management System planning	4.2.3
5.5	Responsibility, authority and communication (title only)	
5.5.1	Responsibility and authority	4.1.2.1
5.5.2	Management representative	4.1.2.3
5.5.3	Internal communication	
5.6	Management review (title only)	
5.6.1	General	4.1.3
5.6.2	Review input	
5.6.3	Review output	
6	Resource management (title only)	
6.1	Provision of resources	4.1.2.2
6.2	Human resources (title only)	
6.2.1	General	4.1.2.2
6.2.2	Competence, awareness and training	4.18
6.3	Infrastructure	4.9
6.4	Work environment	4.9
7	Product realisation (title only)	
7.1	Planning of product realisation	4.2.3, 4.10.1
7.2	Customer-related processes (title only)	

Comparison between ISO 9001:2000 and ISO 9001:1994 *Continued*

Clause No.	ISO 9001:2000 title	ISO 9001:1994 correspondence
7.2.1	Determination of requirements related to the product	4.3.2, 4.4.4
7.2.2	Review of requirements related to the product	4.3.2, 4.3.3, 4.3.4
7.2.3	Customer communication	4.3.2
7.3	Design and development (title only)	
7.3.1	Design and development planning	4.4.2, 4.4.3
7.3.2	Design and development inputs	4.4.4
7.3.3	Design and development outputs	4.4.5
7.3.4	Design and development review	4.4.6
7.3.5	Design and development verification	4.4.7
7.3.6	Design and development validation	4.4.8
7.3.7	Control of design and development changes	4.4.9
7.4	Purchasing (title only)	
7.4.1	Purchasing process	4.6.2
7.4.2	Purchasing information	4.6.3
7.4.3	Verification of purchased product	4.6.4, 4.10.2
7.5	Production and service provision (title only)	
7.5.1	Control of production and service provision	4.9, 4.15.6, 4.19
7.5.2	Validation of processes for production and service provision	4.9

Comparison between ISO 9001:2000 and ISO 9001:1994 *Continued*

Clause No.	ISO 9001:2000 title	ISO 9001:1994 correspondence
7.5.3	Identification and traceability	4.8, 4.10.5, 4.12
7.5.4	Customer property	4.7
7.5.5	Preservation of product	4.15.2, 4.15.3, 4.15.4, 4.15.5
7.6	Control of monitoring and measuring devices	4.11.1, 4.11.2
8	Measurement, analysis and improvement (title only)	
8.1	General	4.10.1, 4.20.1, 4.20.2
8.2	Monitoring and measurement (title only)	
8.2.1	Customer satisfaction	
8.2.2	Internal audit	4.17
8.2.3	Monitoring and measurement of processes	4.17, 4.20.1, 4.20.2
8.2.4	Monitoring and measurement of product	4.10.2, 4.10.3, 4.10.4, 4.10.5, 4.20.1, 4.20.2
8.3	Control of nonconforming product	4.13.1, 4.13.2
8.4	Analysis of data	4.20.1, 4.20.2
8.5	Improvement (title only)	
8.5.1	Continual improvement	4.1.3
8.5.2	Corrective action	4.14.1, 4.14.2
8.5.3	Preventive action	4.14.1, 4.14.3

3.3 Counter-comparison between ISO 9001:1994 and ISO 9001:2000

ISO 9001:1994	ISO 9001:2000
1. Scope	1
2. Normative reference	2
3. Definitions	3
4. Quality system requirements (title only)	
4.1 Management responsibility (title only)	
4.1.1 Quality policy	5.1, 5.3, 5.4.1
4.1.2 Organisation (title only)	
4.1.2.1 Responsibility and authority	5.5.1
4.1.2.2 Resources	6.1, 6.2.1
4.1.2.3 Management representative	5.5.2
4.1.3 Management review	5.61, 8.5.1
4.2 Quality system (title only)	
4.2.1 General	4.1, 4.2.2
4.2.2 Quality system procedures	4.2.1
4.2.3 Quality planning	5.4.2, 7.1
4.3 Contract review (title only)	
4.3.1 General	
4.3.2 Review	5.2, 7.2.1, 7.2.2, 7.2.3
4.3.3 Amendment to a contract	7.2.2

Counter-comparison between ISO 9001:1994 and ISO 9001:2000 *Continued*

ISO 9001:1994	ISO 9001:2000
4.3.4 Records	7.2.2
4.4 Design control (title only)	
4.4.1 General	
4.4.2 Design and development planning	7.3.1
4.4.3 Organisational and technical interfaces	7.3.1
4.4.4 Design input	7.2.1, 7.3.2
4.4.5 Design output	7.3.3
4.4.6 Design review	7.3.4
4.4.7 Design verification	7.3.5
4.4.8 Design validation	7.3.6
4.4.9 Design changes	7.3.7
4.5 Document and data control (title only)	
4.5.1 General	4.2.3
4.5.2 Document and data approval and issue	4.2.3
4.5.3 Document and data changes	4.2.3
4.6 Purchasing (title only)	
4.6.1 General	
4.6.2 Evaluation of subcontractors	7.4.1
4.6.3 Purchasing data	7.4.2
4.6.4 Verification of purchased product	7.4.3

Counter-comparison between ISO 9001:1994 and ISO 9001:2000 *Continued*

ISO 9001:1994	ISO 9001:2000
4.7 Control of customer-supplied product	7.5.4
4.8 Product identification and traceability	7.5.3
4.9 Process control	6.3, 6.4, 7.5.1, 7.5.2
4.10 Inspection and testing (title only)	
4.10.1 General	7.1, 8.1
4.10.2 Receiving inspection and testing	7.4.3, 8.2.4
4.10.3 In-process inspection and testing	8.2.4
4.10.4 Final inspection and testing	8.2.4
4.10.5 Inspection and test records	7.5.3, 8.2.4
4.11 Control of inspection, measuring and test equipment (title only)	
4.11.1 General	7.6
4.11.2 Control procedure	7.6
4.12 Inspection and test status	7.5.3
4.13 Control of nonconforming product (title only)	
4.13.1 General	8.3
4.13.2 Review and disposition of nonconforming product	8.3
4.14 Corrective and preventive action (title only)	
4.14.1 General	8.5.2, 8.5.3
4.14.2 Corrective action	8.5.2

Counter-comparison between ISO 9001:1994 and ISO 9001:2000 *Continued*

ISO 9001:1994	ISO 9001:2000
4.14.3 Preventive action	8.5.3
4.15 Handling, storage, packaging, preservation and delivery (title only)	
4.15.1 General	
4.15.2 Handling	7.5.5
4.15.3 Storage	7.5.5
4.15.4 Packaging	7.5.5
4.15.5 Preservation	7.5.5
4.15.6 Delivery	7.5.1
4.16 Control of quality records	4.2.4
4.17 Internal quality audits	8.2.2, 8.2.3
4.18 Training	6.2.2
4.19 Servicing	7.5.1
4.20 Statistical techniques (title only)	
4.20.1 Identification of need	8.1, 8.2.3, 8.2.4, 8.4
4.20.2 Procedures	8.1, 8.2.3, 8.2.4, 8.4

3.4 Comparison of ISO 9001:2000 headings between CD2, DIS, FDIS and the IS

Clause No.	CD2 ISO 9001:2000 title	Clause No.	DIS ISO 9001:2000 title	Clause No.	FDIS ISO 9001:2000 title	Clause No.	ISO 9001:2000 title
1	Scope	1	Scope	1	Scope	1	Scope
1.2	General	1.1	General	1.1	General	1.1	General
1.3	Reduction in scope	1.2	Permissible exclusions	1.2	Application	1.2	Application
2	Normative references	2	Normative reference	2	Normative reference	2	Normative reference
3	Terms and definitions	3	Terms and definitions	3	Terms and definitions	3	Terms and definitions
		3.1	Product				
4	Quality Management System requirements	4	Quality Management System	4	Quality Management System	4	Quality Management System
		4.1	General requirements	4.1	General requirements	4.1	General requirements
		4.2	General documentation requirements	4.2	Documentation requirements	4.2	Documentation requirements

Comparison of ISO 9001:2000 headings between CD2, DIS, FDIS and the IS *Continued*

CD2 ISO 9001:2000 title	Clause No.	DIS ISO 9001:2000 title	Clause No.	FDIS ISO 9001:2000 title	Clause No.	ISO 9001:2000 title	Clause No.
				General	4.2.1	General	4.2.1
				Quality manual	4.2.2	Quality manual	4.2.2
				Control of documents	4.2.3	Control of documents	4.2.3
				Control of quality records	4.2.4	Control of records	4.2.4
Management responsibility	5	Management responsibility	5	Management responsibility	5	Management responsibility	5
General requirements	5.1	Management commitment	5.1	Management commitment	5.1	Management commitment	5.1
Customer requirements	5.2	Customer focus	5.2	Customer focus	5.2	Customer focus	5.2
Legal requirements	5.3	Quality policy	5.3	Quality policy	5.3	Quality policy	5.3
Policy	5.4						
Planning	5.5	Planning	5.4	Planning	5.4	Planning	5.4

5.5.1	Objectives	5.4.1	Quality objectives	5.4.1	Quality objectives	5.4.1	Quality objectives
5.5.2	Quality planning	5.4.2	Quality planning	5.4.2	Quality management system planning	5.4.2	Quality management system planning
5.6	Quality Management System	5.5	Administration	5.5	Responsibility, authority and communication	5.5	Responsibility, authority and communication
5.6.1	General requirements	5.5.1	General				
5.6.2	Responsibility and authority	5.5.2	Responsibility and authority	5.5.1	Responsibility and authority	5.5.1	Responsibility and authority
5.6.3	Management representative	5.5.3	Management representative	5.5.2	Management representative	5.5.2	Management representative
5.6.4	Internal communications	5.5.4	Internal communication	5.5.3	Internal communication	5.5.3	Internal communication
5.6.5	Quality Manual	5.5.5	Quality Manual		See 4.2.2		See 4.2.2
5.6.6	Control of documents	5.5.6	Control of documents		See 4.2.3		See 4.2.3
5.6.7	Control of records	5.5.7	Control of quality records		See 4.2.4		See 4.2.4

Comparison of ISO 9001:2000 headings between CD2, DIS, FDIS and the IS *Continued*

Clause No.	CD2 ISO 9001:2000 title	Clause No.	DIS ISO 9001:2000 title	Clause No.	FDIS ISO 9001:2000 title	Clause No.	ISO 9001:2000 title
5.7	Management review	5.6	Management review	5.6	Management review	5.6	Management review
		5.6.1	General	5.6.1	General	5.6.1	General
		5.6.2	Review input	5.6.2	Review input	5.6.2	Review input
		5.6.3	Review output	5.6.3	Review output	5.6.3	Review output
6	Resource management	6	Resource management	6	Resource management	6	Resource management
6.1	General requirements	6.1	Provision of resources	6.1	Provision of resources	6.1	Provision of resources
6.2	Human resources	6.2	Human resources	6.2	Human resources	6.2	Human resources
6.2.1	Assignment of personnel	6.2.1	Assignment of personnel	6.2.1	General	6.2.1	General
6.2.2	Competence, training, qualification and awareness	6.2.2	Training, awareness and competency	6.2.2	Competence, awareness and training	6.2.2	Competence, awareness and training
6.3	Information						

6.4	Infrastructure	6.3	Facilities	6.3	Infrastructure	6.3	Infrastructure
6.5	Work environment	6.4	Work environment	6.4	Work environment	6.4	Work environment
7	Product and/or service realisation	7	Product realisation	7	Product realisation	7	Product realisation
7.1	General requirements	7.1	Planning of realisation processes	7.1	Planning of product realisation	7.1	Planning of product realisation
7.2	Customer-related processes	7.2	Customer-related processes	7.2	Customer-related processes	7.2	Customer-related processes
7.2.1	Identification of customer requirements	7.2.1	Identification of customer requirements	7.2.1	Determination of requirements related to the product	7.2.1	Determination of requirements related to the product
7.2.2	Review of customer requirements	7.2.2	Review of customer requirements	7.2.2	Review of requirements related to the product	7.2.2	Review of requirements related to the product
7.2.3	Customer communications	7.2.3	Customer communication	7.2.3	Customer communication	7.2.3	Customer communication
7.3	Design and development	7.3	Design and/or development	7.3	Design and development	7.3	Design and development
7.3.1	General requirements	7.3.1	Design and/or development planning	7.3.1	Design and development planning	7.3.1	Design and development planning

Comparison of ISO 9001:2000 headings between CD2, DIS, FDIS and the IS *Continued*

Clause No.	CD2 ISO 9001:2000 title	Clause No.	DIS ISO 9001:2000 title	Clause No.	FDIS ISO 9001:2000 title	Clause No.	ISO 9001:2000 title
7.3.2	Design and development inputs	7.3.2	Design and/or development inputs	7.3.2	Design and development inputs	7.3.2	Design and development inputs
7.3.3	Design and development outputs	7.3.3	Design and/or development outputs	7.3.3	Design and development outputs	7.3.3	Design and development outputs
7.3.4	Design and development review	7.3.4	Design and/or development review	7.3.4	Design and development review	7.3.4	Design and development review
7.3.5	Design and development verification	7.3.5	Design and/or development verification	7.3.5	Design and development validation	7.3.5	Design and development validation
7.3.6	Design and development validation	7.3.6	Design and/or development validation	7.3.6	Design and development validation	7.3.6	Design and development validation
7.3.7	Control of changes	7.3.7	Control of design and/or development changes	7.3.7	Control of design and development changes	7.3.7	Control of design and development changes
7.4	Purchasing	7.4	Purchasing	7.4	Purchasing	7.4	Purchasing
7.4.1	General requirements	7.4.1	Purchasing control	7.4.1	Purchasing process	7.4.1	Purchasing process

7.4.2	Purchasing information	7.4.2	Purchasing information	7.4.2	Purchasing information	7.4.2	Purchasing information
7.4.3	Verification of purchased product and/or service	7.4.3	Verification of purchased product	7.4.3	Verification of purchased product	7.4.3	Verification of purchased product
7.5	Production and service operations	7.5	Production and service operations	7.5	Production and service provision	7.5	Production and service provision
7.5.1	General requirements	7.5.1	Operations control	7.5.1	Control of production and service provision	7.5.1	Control of production and service provision
				7.5.2	Validation of processes for production and service provision	7.5.2	Validation of processes for production and service provision
7.5.2	Identification and traceability	7.5.2	Identification and traceability	7.5.3	Identification and traceability	7.5.3	Identification and traceability
7.5.3	Customer property	7.5.3	Customer property	7.5.4	Customer property	7.5.4	Customer property
7.5.4	Handling, packaging, storage, preservation and delivery	7.5.4	Preservation of product	7.5.5	Preservation of product	7.5.5	Preservation of product
7.5.5	Validation of processes	7.5.5	Validation of processes		See 7.5.2		See 7.5.2

Comparison of ISO 9001:2000 headings between CD2, DIS, FDIS and the IS *Continued*

Clause No.	CD2 ISO 9001:2000 title	Clause No.	DIS ISO 9001:2000 title	Clause No.	FDIS ISO 9001:2000 title	Clause No.	ISO 9001:2000 title
7.6	Control of measuring and monitoring devices	7.6	Control of measuring and monitoring devices	7.6	Control of monitoring and monitoring devices	7.6	Control of monitoring and measuring devices
8	Measurement, analysis and improvement	8	Measurement, analysis and improvement	8	Measurement, analysis and improvement	8	Measurement, analysis and improvement
8.1	General requirements	8.1	Planning	8.1	General	8.1	General
8.2	Measurement and monitoring	8.2	Measurement and monitoring	8.2	Monitoring and measurement	8.2	Monitoring and measurement
8.2.1	Measurement and monitoring of system performance						
8.2.1.1	Measurement and monitoring of customer satisfaction	8.2.1	Customer satisfaction	8.2.1	Customer satisfaction	8.2.1	Customer satisfaction
8.2.1.2	Internal audit	8.2.2	Internal audit	8.2.2	Internal audit	8.2.2	Internal audit

8.2.2	Measurement and monitoring of processes	8.2.3	Measurement and monitoring of processes	8.2.3	Monitoring and measurement of processes
8.2.3	Measurement and monitoring of product and/or service	8.2.4	Measurement and monitoring of product	8.2.4	Monitoring and measurement of product
8.3	Control of nonconformity	8.3	Control of nonconformity	8.3	Control of nonconforming product
8.3.1	General requirements				
8.3.2	Nonconformity review and disposition				
8.4	Analysis of data for improvement	8.4	Analysis of data	8.4	Analysis of data
8.5	Improvement	8.5	Improvement	8.5	Improvement
8.5.1	General requirements	8.5.1	Planning for continual improvement	8.5.1	Continual improvement
8.5.2	Corrective action	8.5.2	Corrective action	8.5.2	Corrective action
8.5.3	Preventive action	8.5.3	Preventive action	8.5.3	Preventive action

3.5   Complete index for ISO 9001:2000

3.6   ISO 9001:2000 crosscheck to a 1994 QMS

Clause No.	ISO 9001:2000 title	ISO 9001:1994 correspondence	Quality Manual		
			Business Process	Quality Procedure	Work Instruction
1	Scope	1			
1.1	General				
1.2	Application				
2	Normative reference	2			
3	Terms and definitions	3			
4	Quality Management System (title only)				
4.1	General requirements	4.2.1			
4.2	Documentation requirements (title only)				
4.2.1	General	4.2.2			
4.2.2	Quality Manual	4.2.1			
4.2.3	Control of documents	4.5.1, 4.5.2, 4.5.3			

4.2.4	Control of records	4.16			
5	Management responsibility (title only)				
5.1	Management commitment	4.1.1			
5.2	Customer focus	4.3.2			
5.3	Quality policy	4.1.1			
5.4	Planning (title only)				
5.4.1	Quality objectives	4.1.1			
5.4.2	Quality Management System planning	4.2.3			
5.5	Responsibility, authority and communication (title only)				
5.5.1	Responsibility and authority	4.1.2.1			
5.5.2	Management representative	4.1.2.3			
5.5.3	Internal communication				
5.6	Management review (title only)				
5.6.1	General	4.1.3			

ISO 9001:2000 crosscheck to a 1994 QMS *Continued*

Clause No.	ISO 9001:2000 title	ISO 9001:1994 correspondence	Quality Manual		Quality Procedure	Work Instruction
			Business Process			
5.6.2	Review input					
5.6.3	Review output					
6	Resource management (title only)					
6.1	Provision of resources	4.1.2.2				
6.2	Human resources (title only)					
6.2.1	General	4.1.2.2				
6.2.2	Competence, awareness and training	4.18				
6.3	Infrastructure	4.9				
6.4	Work environment	4.9				
7	Product realisation (title only)					
7.1	Planning of product realisation	4.2.3, 4.10.1				

7.2	Customer-related processes (title only)							
7.2.1	Determination of requirements related to the product	4.3.2, 4.4.4						
7.2.2	Review of requirements related to the product	4.3.2, 4.3.3, 4.3.4						
7.2.3	Customer communication	4.3.2						
7.3	Design and development (title only)							
7.3.1	Design and development planning	4.4.2, 4.4.3						
7.3.2	Design and development inputs	4.4.4						
7.3.3	Design and development outputs	4.4.5						
7.3.4	Design and development review	4.4.6						
7.3.5	Design and development verification	4.4.7						
7.3.6	Design and development validation	4.4.8						
7.3.7	Control of design and development changes	4.4.9						
7.4	Purchasing (title only)							
7.4.1	Purchasing process	4.6.2						

ISO 9001:2000 crosscheck to a 1994 QMS *Continued*

Clause No.	ISO 9001:2000 title	ISO 9001:1994 correspondence	Quality Manual		
			Business Process	Quality Procedure	Work Instruction
7.4.2	Purchasing information	4.6.3			
7.4.3	Verification of purchased product	4.6.4, 4.10.2			
7.5	Production and service provision (title only)				
7.5.1	Control of production and service provision	4.9, 4.15.6, 4.19			
7.5.2	Validation of processes for production and service provision	4.9			
7.5.3	Identification and traceability	4.8, 4.10.5, 4.12			
7.5.4	Customer property	4.7			
7.5.5	Preservation of product	4.15.2, 4.15.3, 4.15.4, 4.15.5			
7.6	Control of monitoring and measuring devices	4.11.1, 4.11.2			

8	Measurement, analysis and improvement (title only)					
8.1	General	4.10.1, 4.20.1, 4.20.2				
8.2	Monitoring and measurement (title only)					
8.2.1	Customer satisfaction					
8.2.2	Internal audit	4.17				
8.2.3	Monitoring and measurement of processes	4.17, 4.20.1, 4.20.2				
8.2.4	Monitoring and measurement of product	4.10.2, 4.10.3, 4.10.4, 4.10.5, 4.20.1, 4.20.2				
8.3	Control of nonconforming product	4.13.1, 4.13.2				
8.4	Analysis of data	4.20.1, 4.20.2				
8.5	Improvement (title only)					
8.5.1	Continual improvement	4.1.3				
8.5.2	Corrective action	4.14.1, 4.14.2				
8.5.3	Preventive action	4.14.1, 4.14.3				

3.7   ISO 9001:2000 – explanation and likely documentation

Clause No.	DIS ISO 9001:2000 title	Explanation	Likely documentation
4	Quality Management System		
4.1	General requirements	A definition of the processes necessary to ensure that a product conforms to customer requirements that are capable of being implemented, maintained and improved.	Core Business Processes supplemented by: • Supporting Processes; • QPs; • WIs.
4.2	Documentation requirements		
4.2.1	General	Documented proof of a Quality Management System.	Quality Manual. High level policy statement on organisational objectives and quality policy. Procedures. Quality records.
4.4.2	Quality Manual	A document which describes an organisation's quality policies, procedures and practices that make up the QMS.	A Quality Manual containing everything related to quality controls within an organisation.

4.4.3	Control of documents	How an organisation's documents are approved, issued, numbered etc. How revisions are recorded and implemented and obsolete documents removed.	Document control procedures.
4.4.4	Control of records	What quality records need to be kept to demonstrate conformance with the requirements of an organisation's QMS and how they are identified, stored, protected etc.	Record keeping procedures.
5	Management responsibility	Management responsibility and quality requirements.	Quality Manual.
5.1	Management commitment	A written demonstration of an organisation's commitment to: • sustains and increases customer satisfaction; • establishing quality policies, objectives and planning; • establishing a QMS; • performing management reviews; • ensuring availability of resources; • determining the legal and mandatory requirements its products and/or services have to meet; • continuous improvement.	High-level policy statement on organisational objectives and quality policies. A list of Government regulatory, legal and customer-specific requirements. Procedures describing: • resource management; • contract review procedures; • management reviews; • financial business plan(s).

ISO 9001:2000 – explanation and likely documentation *Continued*

Clause No.	DIS ISO 9001:2000 title	Explanation	Likely documentation
5.2	Customer focus	How an organisation ensures that customer needs, expectations and requirements are determined, fully understood and met.	Procedures describing: • resource management; • contract review procedures; • management reviews; • financial business plan(s).
5.3	Quality policy	How an organisation approaches quality and the requirements for meeting them, ensuring that: • they are appropriate for both customer and an organisation; • there is a commitment to continually meet customer requirements; • these commitments are communicated, understood and implemented throughout an organisation; • there is a commitment for continual improvement.	High-level managerial statement on an organisation's quality policy containing clear responsibilities, training and resources required for each organisational activity.
5.4	Planning	The planning of resources etc. to meet an organisation's overall business objectives.	Quality Manual.

5.4.1	Quality objectives	The quality objectives that an organisation expects to achieve within each function and level of the organisation.	Policy statements defining the objectives of the company and those responsible for achieving the objectives.
5.4.2	Quality Management System planning	The identification and planning of activities and resources required to meet an organisation's quality objectives.	The processes and procedures used by senior management to define and plan the way that the organisation is run.
5.5	Responsibility, authority and communication	How the organisation has documented its QMS.	A Quality Manual containing everything related to quality controls within the organisation.
5.5.1	Responsibility and authority	A definition of the roles, responsibilities, lines of authority, reporting and communication relevant to quality.	Job descriptions and responsibilities. Organisation charts showing lines of communication.
5.5.2	Management representative	The identification and appointment of a 'Quality Manager' with responsibility for the QMS.	Job description and responsibilities. Organisation charts showing lines of communication.
5.5.3	Internal communication	How the requirements of an organisation's QMS are communicated throughout the company.	Team briefings, organisational meetings, notice boards, in-house journals/magazines, audio-visual and other forms of e-information.

ISO 9001:2000 – explanation and likely documentation *Continued*

Clause No.	DIS ISO 9001:2000 title	Explanation	Likely documentation
5.6	Management review	How senior management reviews the QMS to ensure its continued suitability, adequacy and effectiveness, in the context of an organisation's strategic planning cycle.	Procedures concerning: ● process, product and/or service audit procedures; ● customer feedback; ● process and product performance; ● corrective and preventive action; ● supplier performance; ● record keeping.
5.6.1	General	The requirement for management to establish a process for the periodic review of the QMS.	Management review and QMS audit procedures.
5.6.2	Review input	The documents and information required for management reviews.	Results of audits, customer feedback, analysis of process performance and product conformance, corrective and preventive action reports and supplier performance records.
5.6.3	Review output	Result of the review.	Minutes of the meetings where the overall running of the company is discussed.

6	Resource management	A description of resources with regard to training, induction, responsibilities, working environment, equipment requirements, maintenance etc.	QPs, Quality Plans and WIs.
6.1	Provision of resources	How resource needs (i.e. human, materials, equipment, infrastructure) are identified.	Quality Plans identifying the resources required to complete a particular project or activity.
6.2	Human resources	Identification and assignment of human resources to implement and improve the QMS and comply with contract conditions.	QPs, Quality Plans and WIs.
6.2.1	General	How an organisation assigns personnel on the basis of competency, qualification, training, skills and experience relevant to specific tasks.	Job descriptions and responsibilities. Training records. Staff evaluations. Project plans identifying the human resources required to complete the task.
6.2.2	Competence, awareness and training	Documents showing how an organisation selects, trains and assigns personnel to specific tasks.	System level procedures for: • training; • staff evaluations; • review of work assignments; • staff assessments; • records.

ISO 9001:2000 – explanation and likely documentation *Continued*

Clause No.	DIS ISO 9001:2000 title	Explanation	Likely documentation
6.3	Infrastructure	How an organisation defines, provides and maintains the infrastructure requirements to ensure product conformity (e.g. infrastructure, plant, hardware, software, tools and equipment, communication facilities, transport and supporting services, etc).	Policies, procedures and regulatory documents stating the infrastructure requirements of an organisation and/or their customers. Financial documents. Maintenance plans. Project plans identifying the human resources required to complete the task.
6.4	Work environment	How an organisation defines and implements the human and physical factors of the work environment required to ensure product conformity (health and safety, work methods, ethics and ambient working conditions).	Environmental procedures. Project plans. Budgetary and legal processes and procedures.
7	Product realisation	The requirements for process control, purchasing, handling and storage, measuring devices, etc.	Quality Manual and associated Processes, QPs, Quality Plans and WIs.

7.1	Planning of product realisation	The availability of documented plans for all product processes required to realise a product, and the sequences in which they occur.	Process models (flow charts) showing the sequence of activities that an organisation goes through to produce a product. Documented QPs and WIs to ensure that staff work in accordance with requirements. Records that prove the results of process control. Quality Plans.
7.2	Customer-related processes	The identification, review and interaction with customer requirements and customers.	Quality Manual and Quality Plans.
7.2.1	Determination of requirements related to the product	How an organisation determines and implements customer requirements.	Contract review procedures. Regulatory and legal product requirements. Formal contracts.
7.2.2	Review of requirements related to the product	How an organisation reviews product and customer requirements to check that they can actually do the job.	Contract review procedures. Regulatory and legal product requirements. Project plans showing lines of communication with the customer.
7.2.3	Customer communication	How an organisation communicates (i.e. liaises) with their customers, keeps them informed, handles their enquiries, complaints and feedback.	Project plans showing lines of communication with the customer.

ISO 9001:2000 – explanation and likely documentation *Continued*

Clause No.	DIS ISO 9001:2000 title	Explanation	Likely documentation
7.3	Design and development	The control of design and development within an organisation	Processes and procedures for design and development. Design plans.
7.3.1	Design and development planning	How an organisation goes about planning and controlling the design of a product (e.g. design stages, development processes, verification and validation, responsibilities and authorities).	Design and development plans. Procedures detailing the design process and how designs are verified and validated. Risk assessment. Job descriptions and responsibilities.
7.3.2	Design and development inputs	How an organisation identifies the requirements to be met by a product.	Project Plans (detailing policies, standards and specifications, skill requirements). Specifications and tolerances. Regulatory and legal requirements. Information derived from previous (similar) designs or developments. Environmental requirements. Health and safety aspects.

7.3.3	Design and development outputs	How an organisation ensures that the design output meets the design input requirements.	Drawings, schematics, schedules, system specifications, system descriptions etc.
7.3.4	Design and development review	How an organisation evaluates their ability to fulfil product requirements, identify problems and complete follow-up actions.	Procedures detailing how changes are made to designs and how they are approved, recorded and distributed. Design process review procedures. Management reviews and audit procedures. Records.
7.3.5	Design and development verification	How an organisation ensures that product specifications are fulfilled and that the design and development output meets the original input requirements.	Design process review procedures. Procedures for periodic reviews. Records.
7.3.6	Design and development validation	How an organisation ensures that the design is actually capable of doing it intended job.	Procedures for in-process inspection and testing. Final inspection and test. Records.
7.3.7	Control of design and development changes	How changes to a design are approved, together with consideration of how these changes may influence other aspects of the business.	Procedures detailing how changes are made to designs and how they are approved, recorded and distributed. Design process review procedures. Management reviews and audit procedures. Records.

ISO 9001:2000 – explanation and likely documentation *Continued*

Clause No.	DIS ISO 9001:2000 title	Explanation	Likely documentation
7.4	Purchasing	How an organisation controls the purchase of materials, products and/or services from suppliers and third parties.	Documented procedures for purchasing and the evaluation of suppliers.
7.4.1	Purchasing process	The controls that an organisation has in place to ensure purchased products and services are of an acceptable standard.	Approved list of suppliers. Supplier evaluations. Purchasing procedures. Purchase orders.
7.4.2	Purchasing information	The details provided by an organisation when placing an order with a supplier and the approval process for purchasing documentation.	Approved list of suppliers. Supplier evaluations. Purchasing procedures. Purchase orders. Stock control procedures.
7.4.3	Verification of purchased product	The controls that an organisation has in place to ensure that products and services provided by suppliers meet their original requirements.	Approved list of suppliers. Supplier evaluations. Purchasing procedures. Purchase orders. Stock control procedures.

7.5	Production and service provision	The availability of a process to cover all production and service operations.	Documented Processes, QPs and WIs for production and service operations.
7.5.1	Control of production and service provision	The provision of anything required to control production and service operations.	Procedures for the provision of everything necessary for staff to carry out their work. Project plans and resources required to carry out a job.
7.5.2	Validation of production and service provision	How an organisation identifies processes which cannot be verified by subsequent monitoring/testing/inspection (including the validation of these processes to demonstrate their effectiveness).	Procedures for tasks which cannot subsequently be proved to be acceptable.
7.5.3	Identification and traceability	The means by which the status of a product can be identified at all stages of its production/delivery.	Procedures for the provision of everything necessary for staff to carry out their work. Project plans and resources required to carry out a job.
7.5.4	Customer property	How an organisation looks after property provided by a customer, including identification, verification, storage and maintenance.	Procedure for the control of customer property.
7.5.5	Preservation of product	How an organisation looks after its own products (i.e. identification, handling, packaging, storing and protecting) including authorisation of release to a customer.	Product approval procedures. Procedures which ensure the safety and protection of products.

ISO 9001:2000 – explanation and likely documentation *Continued*

Clause No.	DIS ISO 9001:2000 title	Explanation	Likely documentation
7.6	Control of monitoring and measuring devices	The controls that an organisation has in place to ensure that equipment (including software) used for proving conformance to specified requirements is properly maintained, calibrated and verified.	Equipment records of maintenance and calibration. WIs.
8	Measurement, analysis and improvement	The measurement, monitoring, analysis and improvement processes an organisation has in place to ensure that the QMS processes and products conform to requirements.	Procedures for inspection and measurement.
8.1	General	The definitions of procedures to ensure product conformity and product improvement.	Procedures for: • product conformity; • product improvement; • statistical process review.
8.2	Monitoring and measurement	The analysis of customer satisfaction and the control of products and processes.	Procedures for inspection and measurement.
8.2.1	Customer satisfaction	The processes used to establish whether a customer is satisfied with a product.	Procedures for: • customer feedback; • change control; • customer complaints.

8.2.2	Internal audit	The in-house checks made to determine if the QMS is functioning properly, that it continues to comply with the requirements of ISO 9001:2000 and to identify possibilities for improvement.	Audit procedure.
			Audit schedules.
			Audit plans, check sheets and records.
8.2.3	Monitoring and measurement of processes	The methods used to check if processes continue to meet their intended purpose.	Audit schedules.
			Audit plans, check sheets and records.
			Approval procedures for product acceptance.
			Processes for failure cost analysis, conformity, nonconformity, lifecycle approach, self-assessment.
			Compliance with environmental and safety policies, laws, regulations and standards.
			Procedures for testing and monitoring processes.
			Performance and product measurement procedures.

ISO 9001:2000 – explanation and likely documentation *Continued*

Clause No.	DIS ISO 9001:2000 title	Explanation	Likely documentation
8.2.3	Monitoring and measurement of product	How an organisation measures and monitors that product characteristics meet the customer's specified requirements.	Audit schedules. Audit plans, check sheets and records. Approval procedures for product acceptance. Processes for failure cost analysis, conformity, nonconformity, lifecycle approach, self-assessment. Compliance with environmental and safety policies, laws, regulations and standards. Procedures for testing and monitoring processes. Performance and product measurement procedures. Supplier approval procedures.

8.3	Control of nonconforming product	The methods used to prevent the use or delivery of nonconforming products and to decide what to do with a nonconforming product.	Documented procedure to identify and control the use and delivery of nonconforming products. Approval procedures. Quarantine procecures. Change control procedure. Corrective and preventive action procedures. Audits.
8.4	Analysis of data	The methods used to review data that will determine the effectiveness of the QMS, especially with regard to customer satisfaction, conformance to customer requirements and the performance of processes and products.	Any data or statistics produced as a result of audits, customer satisfaction surveys, complaints, nonconformances, supplier evaluations etc.
8.5	Improvement	How an organisation controls corrective and preventive actions and plans for ongoing process and product improvement.	Documented procedures for: • corrective action; • preventive action; • product/process improvement; • customer complaints/feedback. Nonconformity reports. Management reviews. Staff suggestions scheme.

ISO 9001:2000 – explanation and likely documentation *Continued*

Clause No.	DIS ISO 9001:2000 title	Explanation	Likely documentation
8.5.1	Continual improvement	How an organisation goes about continually improving its QMS.	Procedures, minutes of meetings where improvement to the organisation's business is discussed. Management reviews.
8.5.2	Corrective action	What an organisation does to identify and put right nonconformities.	Process for eliminating causes of nonconformity. Documented complaints. Complaints procedure. Staff suggestions scheme.
8.5.3	Preventive action	The proactive methods an organisation employs to prevent nonconformities from happening in the first place.	Process for the prevention of nonconformity. Documented complaints. Complaints procedure. Staff suggestions scheme.

3.8 Audit check sheet

4. QUALITY MANAGEMENT SYSTEM

4.1 General requirements

Item	Requirement	Currently met? Yes/No	Document	Remarks
1.	Has a Quality Management System been established in accordance with the requirements of ISO 9001:2000?			
2.	Is the QMS:			
	• documented?			
	• implemented?			
	• maintained?			
	• continually improved?			
3.	Does the organisation have all the documents necessary to ensure the effective operation and control of its processes?			

General requirements *Continued*

Item	Requirement	Currently met? Yes/No	Document	Remarks
4.	Has the organisation:			
	● identified the processes needed for the QMS?			
	● determined the sequence and interaction of these processes?			
	● determined the criteria and methods required to ensure the effective operation and control of these processes?			
	● ensured that information necessary to support the monitoring and operation of these processes is available?			
5.	Does the organisation measure, monitor and analyse these processes?			
6.	Is the necessary action implemented to achieve planned results and continual improvement?			
7.	Does the organisation manage these processes in accordance with the requirements of ISO 9001:2000?			

4.2 Document requirements

4.2.1 General

Item	Requirement	Currently met? Yes/No	Document	Remarks
8.	Does the QMS include:			
	• statements on quality policy and quality objectives?			
	• a quality manual?			
	• documented procedures?			
	• quality records?			

4.2.2 Quality manual

Item	Requirement	Currently met? Yes/No	Document	Remarks
9.	Has the organisation established and maintained a Quality Manual?			
10.	Is it controlled?			
11.	Does it include details of:			
	● the scope of the QMS?			
	● justifications for any exclusions from the ISO 9001:2000 requirements?			
	● associated documented procedures (or reference to them)?			
	● the sequence and interaction of processes?			

4.2.3   Control of documents

Item	Requirement	Currently met? Yes/No	Document	Remarks
12.	Has the organisation established a documented procedure to control QMS documents?			
13.	Does this procedure include methods for:			
	• controlling distribution?			
	• approving of documents prior to issue?			
	• reviewing, updating and re-approving documents?			
	• identifying the current revision status of documents?			
	• ensuring that relevant versions of all applicable documents are available at points of use?			
	• ensuring that documents remain legible, readily identifiable and retrievable?			
	• identifying, distributing and controlling of documents from an external source?			
	• controlling obsolete documents?			
	• the identification and control of obsolete documents that have been retained for any purpose?			

4.2.4   Control of records

Item	Requirement	Currently met? Yes/No	Document	Remarks
14.	Does the organisation control records?			
15.	Do these records provide evidence of:			
	• the organisation's conformance to the ISO 9001:2000 requirements?			
	• the effective operation of the QMS?			
16.	Does the organisation have a documented procedure for records covering:			
	• identification?			
	• storage?			
	• retrieval?			
	• protection?			
	• retention time?			
	• disposition?			

5. MANAGEMENT RESPONSIBILITY

Item	Requirement	Currently met? Yes/No	Document	Remarks
17.	Does the organisation demonstrate its commitment to developing, establishing and improving the QMS through:			
	• management commitment?			
	• determining customer requirements and achieving customer satisfaction?			
	• a quality policy?			
	• quality objectives and quality planning?			
	• providing all the necessary resources to administer the QMS?			
	• regularly reviewing the QMS?			

5.1 Management commitment

Item	Requirement	Currently met? Yes/No	Document	Remarks
18.	Does the organisation demonstrate its commitment to developing, establishing and improving the QMS?			
19.	Does the organisation:			
	● ensure that all personnel are aware of the importance of meeting customer, regulatory and legal requirements?			
	● establish the quality policy and quality objectives?			
	● conduct management reviews?			
	● ensure the availability of necessary resources?			

5.2 Customer focus

Item	Requirement	Currently met? Yes/No	Document	Remarks
20.	Does the organisation ensure that customer needs and expectations are determined?			
21.	Are these customer needs and expectations converted into requirements?			
22.	Does the organisation ensure that customer requirements are fulfilled?			

5.3 Quality policy

Item	Requirement	Currently met? Yes/No	Document	Remarks
23.	Is the organisation's quality policy:			
	• controlled?			
	• appropriate?			
	• committed to meeting requirements?			
	• communicated and understood throughout the company?			
	• capable of continual improvement?			
	• a framework for establishing and reviewing quality objectives?			
	• regularly reviewed for continued suitability?			

5.4 Planning

Item	Requirement	Currently met? Yes/No	Document	Remarks
24.	Is the organisation's quality planning documented?			
25.	Does it include:			
	• quality objectives?			
	• resources?			

5.4.1 Quality objectives

Item	Requirement	Currently met? Yes/No	Document	Remarks
26.	Has the organisation established quality objectives for each relevant function and level within the company?			
27.	Are the organisation's quality objectives measurable and consistent with quality policy?			
28.	Do they include:			
	• a commitment for continual improvement?			
	• product requirements?			

5.4.2 Quality Management System planning

Item	Requirement	Currently met? Yes/No	Document	Remarks
29.	Does the organisation's quality planning cover:			
	• the processes required in the QMS (as mentioned in section 4)?			
	• any permissible exclusions (to the requirements of ISO 9001:2000)?			
	• the requirements for continual improvement?			
	• the requirements for change control?			
30.	Does the organisation's quality planning ensure that the QMS is maintained during this change?			

5.5 Responsibility, authority and communication

Item	Requirement	Currently met? Yes/No	Document	Remarks
31.	Is the administration of the organisation's QMS documented?			
32.	Does it cover:			
	• responsibilities and authorities?			
	• management representative's duties?			
	• internal communication?			
	• the Quality Manual?			
	• control of documents?			
	• control of quality records?			

5.5.1 Responsibility and authority

Item	Requirement	Currently met? Yes/No	Document	Remarks
33.	Are the functions and inter-relationships of all the organisation staff defined?			
34.	Are the responsibilities and authorities of all the organisation staff defined?			

5.5.2 Management representative

Item	Requirement	Currently met? Yes/No	Document	Remarks
35.	Has the organisation management member(s) been appointed as management representative(s)?			
36.	Does the management representative(s):			
	• ensure that the QMS processes are established, implemented and maintained?			
	• report (to top management) on the performance (and methods for improving) the QMS?			
	• promote awareness of customer requirements throughout the organisation?			
	• liaise with external parties on all matters relating the QMS?			

5.5.3 Internal communication

Item	Requirement	Currently met? Yes/No	Document	Remarks
37.	Does the organisation ensure that there are lines of communication between all members of staff to ensure the effectiveness of the QMS processes?			

5.6 Management review

Item	Requirement	Currently met? Yes/No	Document	Remarks
38.	Does the organisation top management regularly review the QMS at planned intervals?			

5.6.1 General

Item	Requirement	Currently met? Yes/No	Document	Remarks
39.	Does the QMS review cover the continuing suitability, adequacy and effectiveness of the QMS?			
40.	Does the review evaluate the need for changes?			
41.	Does the review			
	● quality policy?			
	● quality objectives?			

5.6.2 Review input

Item	Requirement	Currently met? Yes/No	Document	Remarks
42.	Does the management review include:			
	• internal audit results?			
	• external and third party audit results?			
	• customer feedback?			
	• process performance?			
	• product conformance?			
	• preventive and corrective actions that have been implemented?			
	• outstanding preventive and corrective actions?			
	• results from previous management reviews?			
	• changes that could affect the QMS?			

5.6.3 Review output

Item	Requirement	Currently met? Yes/No	Document	Remarks
43.	Do the outputs of management reviews include recommendations for:			
	• the improvement of the QMS and its processes?			
	• the improvement of product related to customer requirements?			
	• confirming and establishing resource needs?			
44.	Are the results of management reviews recorded?			

6. RESOURCE MANAGEMENT

Item	Requirement	Currently met? Yes/No	Document	Remarks
45.	Has the organisation documented procedures that adequately cover the requirements for:			
	● training?			
	● induction?			
	● responsibilities?			
	● working environment?			
	● equipment requirements?			
	● maintenance?			

6.1 Provision of resources

Item	Requirement	Currently met? Yes/No	Document	Remarks
46.	Does the organisation provide the resources required to:			
	• implement and improve the QMS processes?			
	• ensure customer satisfaction?			

6.2 Human resources

Item	Requirement	Currently met? Yes/No	Document	Remarks
47.	Has the organisation established procedures for:			
	• the assignment of personnel?			
	• training, awareness and competency?			

6.2.1 General

Item	Requirement	Currently met? Yes/No	Document	Remarks
48.	Are staff responsibilities defined in the QMS?			
49.	Are those members of staff assigned responsibilities based on their:			
	• competency?			
	• applicable education?			
	• training?			
	• skills?			
	• experience?			

6.2.2 Competence, awareness and training

Item	Requirement	Currently met? Yes/No	Document	Remarks
50.	Does the organisation:			
51.	identify training requirements?			
52.	provide appropriate training?			
53.	evaluate the training provided?			
54.	Does the organisation ensure that all their staff appreciate the relevance and importance of their activities and how they contribute towards achieving quality objectives?			
55.	Does the organisation keep staff records covering education, experience, qualifications, training, etc.).			

6.3 Infrastructure

Item	Requirement	Currently met? Yes/No	Document	Remarks
56.	Does the organisation identify, provide and maintain the necessary:			
	● workspace and associated facilities?			
	● equipment, hardware and software?			
	● supporting services?			

6.4 Work environment

Item	Requirement	Currently met? Yes/No	Document	Remarks
57.	Does the organisation identify and manage the work environment (including human and physical factors) to ensure conformity of product?			

7. PRODUCT REALISATION

Item	Requirement	Currently met? Yes/No	Document	Remarks
58.	Has the organisation established the processes necessary to achieve the product?			

7.1 Planning of product realisation

Item	Requirement	Currently met? Yes/No	Document	Remarks
59.	Have the sequence of processes and sub-processes required to achieve the product been documented and planned?			
60.	Within this sequence of processes and sub-processes, has the following been determined:			
	● the quality objectives for the product, project or contract?			
	● product-specific processes, documentation, resources and facilities?			
	● verification and validation activities?			
	● criteria for acceptability?			
	● required records?			

7.2 Customer-related processes

Item	Requirement	Currently met? Yes/No	Document	Remarks
61.	Has the organisation established procedures for the:			
	• identification of customer requirements?			
	• review of product requirements?			
	• customer communication?			

7.2.1 Determination of requirements related to the product

Item	Requirement	Currently met? Yes/No	Document	Remarks
62.	Has the organisation established a process for identifying customer requirements?			
63.	Does this process determine:			
	• customer-specified product requirements (e.g. availability, delivery and support)?			
	• non-specified customer requirements (e.g. those affecting the product)?			
	• mandatory requirements such as regulatory and legal obligations?			

7.2.2   Review of requirements related to the product

Item	Requirement	Currently met? Yes/No	Document	Remarks
64.	Has the organisation established a process for ensuring that product requirements have been fully established?			
65.	Does the process ensure that (prior to submission of tender or acceptance of contract):			
	• all customer requirements (plus any additional requirements determined by the organisation) have been defined and can be met?			
	• where no written requirements are available, that verbal customer requirements are confirmed before contract acceptance?			
	• any contract or order requirements differing from those previously express (e.g. in a tender or quotation) are resolved?			
	• the organisation has the ability to meet the defined requirements?			

7.2.3 Customer communication

Item	Requirement	Currently met? Yes/No	Document	Remarks
66.	Has the organisation established processes for:			
	• providing customers with product information?			
	• handling customer enquiries, contracts or orders (including amendments)?			
	• customer feedback and/or customer complaints?			

7.3 Design and development

Item	Requirement	Currently met? Yes/No	Document	Remarks
67.	Has the organisation a process and adequate procedures for their design and development activities?			

7.3.1 Design and development planning

Item	Requirement	Currently met? Yes/No	Document	Remarks
68.	Does the organisation plan and control design and development of the product by means of processes?			
69.	Do these processes include:			
	• stage review, verification and validation activities?			
	• identification of responsibilities and authorities?			
	• management of the interfaces between different groups that may be involved?			
	• provision of effective communication and clarity of responsibilities?			
	• product and planning reviews?			

7.3.2   Design and development inputs

Item	Requirement	Currently met? Yes/No	Document	Remarks
70.	Does the organisation define and document product requirement inputs?			
71.	Do these input requirements include:			
	• function and performance requirements?			
	• applicable regulatory and legal requirements?			
	• applicable requirements derived from previous similar designs?			
	• any other requirements essential for design and development?			
72.	Are inadequate, incomplete, ambiguous or conflicting input requirements resolved?			

7.3.3 Design and development outputs

Item	Requirement	Currently met? Yes/No	Document	Remarks
73.	Does the organisation define and document product outputs?			
74.	Are products approved prior to release?			
75.	Does the design and development output:			
	● meet the design and development input requirements?			
	● provide appropriate information for production and service operations?			
	● contain or make reference to product acceptance criteria?			
	● define the characteristics of the product that are essential to its safe and proper use?			

7.3.4 Design and development review

Item	Requirement	Currently met? Yes/No	Document	Remarks
76.	Are systematic reviews of the design and development carried out at suitable stages?			
77.	Does the review:			
	• evaluate the ability of the product to fulfil the requirements?			
	• identify problems and propose solutions?			
	• include representatives from the functions concerned with the design and development stage being reviewed?			
78.	Are follow-up actions from the reviews recorded?			

7.3.5 Design and development verification

Item	Requirement	Currently met? Yes/No	Document	Remarks
79.	Does the organisation verify that the design output meets the design and development input?			
80.	Are these results and any necessary subsequent follow-up actions recorded?			

7.3.6 Design and development validation

Item	Requirement	Currently met? Yes/No	Document	Remarks
81.	Does the organisation validate that the product is capable of meeting the requirements of intended use?			
82.	Are these results and any necessary subsequent follow-up actions recorded?			
83.	Wherever applicable, is the validation completed prior to the delivery or implementation of the product?			
84.	If full validation is impractical prior to delivery or implementation of the product, is a partial validation performed to the maximum extent applicable?			

7.3.7 Control of design and development changes

Item	Requirement	Currently met? Yes/No	Document	Remarks
85.	Are all design and development changes identified, documented and controlled?			
86.	Does the organisation:			
	• evaluate the effect of the changes on constituent parts and delivered products?			
	• verify, validate and approve these changes before implementation?			
87.	Are these results and any necessary subsequent follow-up actions recorded?			

7.4 Purchasing

Item	Requirement	Currently met? Yes/No	Document	Remarks
88.	Does the organisation have processes for:			
	• purchasing control?			
	• purchasing information?			
	• verification of purchased product?			

7.4.1 Purchasing process

Item	Requirement	Currently met? Yes/No	Document	Remarks
89.	Does the organisation have a process to ensure purchased products conform to requirements?			
90.	Does the organisation evaluate and select suppliers?			
91.	Is this evaluation and selection criteria defined?			
92.	Are these results and any necessary subsequent follow-up actions recorded?			
93.	Does the organisation complete periodic inspections and examinations of purchasing processes?			

7.4.2 Purchasing information

Item	Requirement	Currently met? Yes/No	Document	Remarks
94.	Does the organisation have documentation describing:			
	• the product to be purchased?			
	• requirements for approval or qualification (i.e. product, procedures, processes, equipment and personnel)?			
	• QMS requirements?			
95.	Does the organisation ensure the adequacy of the specified requirements contained in the purchasing documents prior to their release?			

7.4.3 Verification of purchased product

Item	Requirement	Currently met? Yes/No	Document	Remarks
96.	Does the organisation identify and implement the activities necessary for the verification of a purchased product?			
97.	Are these verification arrangements specified by the organisation or its customer if verification is to be carried out at the supplier's premises?			
98.	Is the method of product release specified in the purchasing documents if verification is to be carried out at the supplier's premises?			

7.5 Production and service provision

Item	Requirement	Currently met? Yes/No	Document	Remarks
99.	Does the organisation have procedures for the control of:			
	• production and service operations?			
	• identification and traceability?			
	• customer property?			
	• preservation of product?			
	• validation of processes?			

7.5.1   Control of production and service provision

Item	Requirement	Currently met? Yes/No	Document	Remarks
100.	Does the organisation control production and service operations?			
101.	Is this achieved through:			
	● information concerning the characteristics of the product?			
	● appropriate work instructions?			
	● the use and maintenance of suitable equipment for production and service operations?			
	● the availability and use of measuring and monitoring devices?			
	● the capability of implementing monitoring activities?			
	● processes to cover the release, delivery and post-delivery activities?			

7.5.2 Validation of processes for production and service provision

Item	Requirement	Currently met? Yes/No	Document	Remarks
102.	Does the organisation validate any production and service processes to demonstrate the ability of the processes to achieve planned results (where the resulting output cannot be verified by subsequent measurement or monitoring)?			
103.	Does this validation demonstrate the ability of the processes to achieve planned results?			
104.	Does the validation include:			
	• qualification of processes?			
	• qualification of equipment and personnel?			
	• use of defined methodologies and procedures?			
	• requirements for records?			
	• re-validation?			
105.	Does this validation include any processes where deficiencies may become apparent only after the product is in use or the service has been delivered?			

7.5.3 Identification and traceability

Item	Requirement	Currently met? Yes/No	Document	Remarks
106.	Does the organisation have procedures available to identify the product throughout production and service operations?			
107.	Is the product status identifiable with respect to measurement and monitoring requirements?			
108.	When traceability is a requirement, does the organisation control and record the unique identification of a product?			

7.5.4 Customer property

Item	Requirement	Currently met? Yes/No	Document	Remarks
109.	Does the organisation exercise care with customer property?			
110.	Does the organisation verify, protect and maintain customer property provided for use or incorporated into a product?			
111.	Are records maintained of any customer property that is lost, damaged or otherwise found to be unsuitable for use?			

7.5.5 Preservation of product

Item	Requirement	Currently met? Yes/No	Document	Remarks
112.	Does the organisation have set procedures for the identification, handling, packaging, storage and protection of products during internal processing and delivery to the intended destination?			

7.6 Control of monitoring and measuring devices

Item	Requirement	Currently met? Yes/No	Document	Remarks
113.	Where applicable, are measuring and monitoring devices:			
	• calibrated and adjusted periodically or prior to use, against devices traceable to International or national standards?			
	• safeguarded from adjustments that would invalidate the calibration?			
	• protected from damage and deterioration during handling, maintenance and storage?			

Control of monitoring and measuring devices *Continued*

Item	Requirement	Currently met? Yes/No	Document	Remarks
114.	Are the results of the calibration recorded?			
115.	Is the validity of previous results re-assessed if they are subsequently found to be out of calibration, and corrective action taken?			
116.	If software is used for measuring and monitoring, has it been validated prior to use?			

8.   MEASUREMENT, ANALYSIS AND IMPROVEMENT

Item	Requirement	Currently met? Yes/No	Document	Remarks
117.	Does the organisation define the activities needed to measure and monitor:			
	● product conformity?			
	● product improvement?			

8.1 General

Item	Requirement	Currently met? Yes/No	Document	Remarks
118.	Has the organisation defined, planned and implemented measures and monitoring activities need to assure product continuity and achieve improvement?			
119.	Does this include the determination of the need for, and the use of, applicable methodologies including statistical techniques?			

8.2 Monitoring and measurement

Item	Requirement	Currently met? Yes/No	Document	Remarks
120.	Has the organisation procedures available to:			
	● ensure customer satisfaction?			
	● control internal audits?			
	● ensure effective measurement and monitoring of products and processes?			

8.2.1 *Customer satisfaction*

Item	Requirement	Currently met? Yes/No	Document	Remarks
121.	Does the organisation monitor information on customer satisfaction?			
122.	Does the organisation monitor information on customer dissatisfaction?			
123.	Are the methods and measures for obtaining such information defined?			
124.	Are these methods and measures utilised as part of the performance measurements of the QMS?			

8.2.2 Internal audit

Item	Requirement	Currently met? Yes/No	Document	Remarks
125.	Does the organisation conduct periodic internal audits?			
126.	Do these audits determine whether the QMS:			
	• conforms to the requirements of ISO 9001:2000?			
	• has been effectively implemented and maintained?			
127.	Are audits only carried out by personnel who are not associated with the activity or department being audited?			
128.	Are the audits planned to take into account:			
	• the status and importance of the activities and areas to be audited?			
	• the results of previous audits?			

Internal audit *Continued*

Item	Requirement	Currently met? Yes/No	Document	Remarks
129.	Are the audit scope, frequency and methodologies defined?			
130.	Does the organisation have a documented procedure for audits that includes:			
	• the responsibilities and requirements for conducting audits?			
	• the method for recording results?			
	• the method for reporting to management?			
131.	Does management take timely corrective action on deficiencies found during an audit?			
132.	Do these follow-up actions include the verification of the implementation of corrective action and the reporting of verification results?			

8.2.3 Monitoring and measurement of processes

Item	Requirement	Currently met? Yes/No	Document	Remarks
133.	Does the organisation apply suitable methods for the measurement and monitoring of processes:			
	● to meet customer requirements?			
	● to confirm the process's continuing ability to satisfy its intended purpose?			

8.3.4 Monitoring and measurement of product

Item	Requirement	Currently met? Yes/No	Document	Remarks
134.	Does the organisation apply suitable methods to measure and monitor the characteristics of the product at appropriate stages of the product realisation process?			
135.	Is there documented evidence of conformity with the acceptance criteria?			
136.	Are the responsibilities and authorities defined with regard to release of product?			
137.	Does the organisation ensure that the product is not released or the service delivered until all the specified activities have been satisfactorily completed (unless otherwise approved by the customer)?			

8.3 Control of nonconforming product

Item	Requirement	Currently met? Yes/No	Document	Remarks
138.	Has the organisation defined a procedure for the control of nonconformities?			
139.	Does this procedure ensure that:			
	• products which do not conform to requirements are prevented from unintended use or delivery?			
	• nonconforming products that have been corrected are subject to reverification to demonstrate conformity?			
	• nonconforming products detected after delivery or use are either corrected or removed from service?			
140.	Is there provision for the notification of the customer, end user, regulatory or other body when required?			

8.4   Analysis of data

Item	Requirement	Currently met? Yes/No	Document	Remarks
141.	Does the organisation collect and analyse data to determine the suitability and effectiveness of the QMS and to identify improvements that can be made?			
142.	Does the organisation analyse the data to provide information on:			
	• customer satisfaction and/or dissatisfaction?			
	• conformance to customer requirements?			
	• the characteristics of processes, products and their trends?			
	• suppliers?			

8.5   Improvement

Item	Requirement	Currently met? Yes/No	Document	Remarks
143.	Does the organisation have procedures available for:			
	• planning continual improvement?			
	• corrective action?			
	• preventive action?			

8.5.1   Continual improvement

Item	Requirement	Currently met? Yes/No	Document	Remarks
144.	Does the organisation plan and manage the processes necessary for the continual improvement of the QMS?			
145.	Is the continual improvement of the QMS facilitated by the use of:			
	• the quality policy?			
	• quality objectives?			
	• audit results?			
	• analysis of data?			
	• corrective and preventive action?			
	• management reviews?			
	• concessions and approvals?			
	• concession scheme?			
	• defects and defect reports?			
	• bonded store?			

8.5.2   Corrective action

Item	Requirement	Currently met? Yes/No	Document	Remarks
146.	Has the organisation a documented procedure to enable corrective action to be taken to eliminate the cause of nonconformities and prevent recurrence?			
147.	Does this procedure define the requirements for:			
	• identification of nonconformities (including customer complaints)?			
	• determining the causes of nonconformities?			
	• evaluating the need for action to ensure that nonconformities do not recur?			
	• determining and implementing the corrective action needed?			
	• ensuring results of action taken are recorded?			
	• reviewing the corrective action taken?			

8.5.3 *Preventive action*

Item	Requirement	Currently met? Yes/No	Document	Remarks
148.	Has the organisation a documented procedure to enable preventive action to be taken to eliminate the causes of potential nonconformities and prevent occurrence?			
149.	Does this procedure define the requirements for:			
	● identification of potential nonconformities and their causes?			
	● determining and implementing the preventive action needed?			
	● ensuring results of action taken are recorded?			
	● reviewing the preventive action taken?			

3.9   Stage audit check sheets

DESIGN STAGE

Item		Related Item		Remark	Yes/No	Remarks
1	Requirements	1.1	Information	Has the customer fully described his requirement?		
				Has the customer any mandatory requirements?		
				Are the customer's requirements fully understood by all members of the design team?		
				Is there a need to have further discussions with the customer?		
				Are other suppliers or subcontractors involved? If yes, who is the prime contractor?		
		1.2	Standards	What international standards need to be observed? Are they available?		

Design Stage *Continued*

	Item	Related Item		Remark	Yes/No	Remarks
1	Requirements *Continued*	1.2	Standards *Continued*	What national standards need to be observed? Are they available?		
				What other information and procedures are required? Are they available?		
		1.3	Procedures	Are there any customer-supplied drawings, sketches or plans? Have they been registered?		
2	Quality Procedures	2.1	Procedures Manual	Is one available? Does it contain detailed procedures and instructions for the control of all drawings within the drawing office?		
		2.2	Planning implementation and production	Is the project split into a number of Work Packages? If so: ● are the various Work Packages listed?		

3	Drawings		• have Work Package Leaders been nominated? • is their task clear? • is their task achievable?		
			Is a time plan available? Is it up to date? Regularly maintained? Relevant to the task?		
		3.1	Identification	Are all drawings identified by a unique number?		
				Is the numbering system strictly controlled?		
		3.2	Cataloguing	Is a catalogue of drawings maintained? Is this catalogue regularly reviewed and up to date?		
		3.3	Amendments and modifications	Is there a procedure for authorising the issue of amendments, changes to drawings?		
				Is there a method for withdrawing and disposing of obsolete drawings?		

Design Stage *Continued*

	Item		Related Item	Remark	Yes/No	Remarks
4	Components	4.1	Availability	Are complete lists of all the relevant components available?		
		4.2	Adequacy	Are the selected components currently available and adequate for the task? If not, how long will they take to procure? Is this acceptable?		
		4.3	Acceptability	If alternative components have to be used are they acceptable to the task?		
5	Records	5.1	Failure reports	Has the Design Office access to all records, failure reports and other relevant data?		
		5.2	Reliability data	Is reliability data correctly stored, maintained and analysed?		

	5.3	Graphs, diagrams, plans	In addition to drawings, is there a system for the control of all graphs, tables, plans etc.? Are CAD facilities available? (If so, go to 6.1)		
6		Reviews and Audits			
	6.1	Computers	If a processor is being used: • are all the design office personnel trained in its use? • are regular back-ups taken? • is there an anti-virus system in place?		
	6.2	Manufacturing division	Is a close relationship being maintained between the design office and the manufacturing division?		
	6.3		Is notice being taken of the manufacturing division's exact requirements, their problems and their choices of components etc.?		

MANUFACTURING STAGE

	Item	Related Item	Remark	Yes/No	Remarks
1	Degree of quality	1.1 Quality control procedures	Are quality control procedures available?		
			Are they relevant to the task?		
			Are they understood by all members of the manufacturing team?		
			Are they regularly reviewed and up to date?		
			Are they subject to control procedures?		
		1.2 Quality control checks	What quality checks are being observed?		
			Are they relevant?		
			Are there laid down procedures for carrying out these checks?		
			Are they available?		
			Are they regularly updated?		

2	Reliability of product design			
		2.1	Statistical data	Is there a system for predicting the reliability of the product's design?
				Is sufficient statistical data available to be able to estimate the actual reliability of the design, before a product is manufactured?
				Is the appropriate engineering data available?
		2.2	Components and parts	Are the reliability ratings of recommended parts and components available?
				Are probability methods used to examine the reliability of a proposed design?
				If so, have these checks revealed design deficiencies such as:
				Assembly errors?
				Operator learning, motivational, or fatigue factors?
				Latent defects?
				Improper part selection?
				(Note: If necessary, use additional sheets to list actions taken)

ACCEPTANCE STAGE

	Item	Related Item		Remark	Yes/No	Remarks
1	Product performance			Does the product perform to the required function? If not what has been done about it?		
2	Quality level	2.1	Workmanship	Does the workmanship of the product fully meet the level of quality required or stipulated by the user?		
		2.2	Tests	Is the product subjected to environmental tests? If so, which ones?		
				Is the product field tested as a complete system? If so, what were the results?		

3	Reliability				
	3.1	Probability function	Are individual components and modules environmentally tested? If so, how?		
	3.2	Failure rate	Is the product's reliability measured in terms of probability function? If so, what were the results?		
			Is the product's reliability measured in terms of failure rate? If so, what were the results?		
	3.3	Mean time between failures	Is the product's reliability measured in terms of mean time between failure? If so, what were the results?		

IN-SERVICE STAGE

	Item	Related Item	Remark	Yes/No	Remarks
1	System reliability	1.1	Product basic design	Are statistical methods being used to prove the product's basic design?		
				If so, are they adequate?		
				Are the results recorded and available?		
				What other methods are used to prove the product's basic design?		
				Are these methods appropriate?		
2	Equipment reliability	2.1	Personnel	Are there sufficient trained personnel to carry out the task?		
				Are they sufficiently motivated?		
				If not, what is the problem?		
			2.1.1	Operators	Have individual job descriptions been developed?		
				Are they readily available?		
				Are all operators capable of completing their duties?		
			2.1.2	Training	Do all personnel receive appropriate training?		

	Is a continuous on-the-job training (OJT) programme available to all personnel? If not, why not?						
2.2	Product dependability	What proof is there that the product is dependable? How is product dependability proved? Is this sufficient for the customer?					
2.3	Component reliability	Has the reliability of individual component been considered? Does the reliability of individual components exceed the overall system reliability?					
2.4	Faulty operating procedures	Are operating procedures available? Are they appropriate to the task? Are they regularly reviewed?					
2.5	Operational abuses	Are there any obvious operational abuses? If so, what are they? How can they be overcome?					

In-Service Stage *Continued*

	Item	Related Item		Remark	Yes/No	Remarks
2	Equipment reliability *Continued*	2.5.1	Extended duty cycle	Do the staff have to work shifts?		
				If so, are they allowed regular breaks from their work?		
				Is there a senior shift worker?		
				If so, are his duties and responsibilities clearly defined?		
				Are computers used?		
				If so, are screen filters available?		
				Do the operators have keyboard wrist rests?		
		2.5.2	Training	Do the operational staff receive regular on-the-job training?		
				Is there any need for additional in-house or external training?		
3	Design capability	3.1	Faulty operating procedures	Are there any obvious faulty operating procedures?		
				Can the existing procedures be improved upon?		

3.10   Additional (general purpose) audit checks

Note: Although these are primarily intended for audits of existing ISO 9001:1994, ISO 9002:1994 and/or ISO 9003:1994 Quality Management Systems, they may, nevertheless, prove useful as a general purpose set of checks for ISO 9001:2000 compliant systems.

1.   Management Responsibility

Item	Requirement	Currently met? Yes/No	Document	Remarks
1.	How often is the company quality policy reviewed and revised, by whom, and is he/she suitably placed in the company to do so?			
2.	Who determines that the quality policies are compatible with other company objectives?			
3.	Who is responsible for ensuring that the quality policy is understood and implemented?			
4.	How is the quality policy used to set objectives and who is involved in the decision-making?			

Management Responsibility *Continued*

Item	Requirement	Currently met? Yes/No	Document	Remarks
5.	Who is the Management Representative, who has the defined authority to implement quality policies and objectives and has he/she sufficient authority to fulfil this task?			
6.	How often and by whom is the QMS reviewed for adequacy and how is its performance quantified and reported?			
7.	Who is responsible for identifying, reviewing and recommending solutions to minimise or prevent quality-related problems and how is this achieved?			
8.	Who reviews quality objectives to ensure that they are achieved or instigates action in order to implement them?			
9.	Is the review effective and how is action monitored?			
10.	Are there records that give evidence of the review process?			

2. QMS

Item	Requirement	Currently met? Yes/No	Document	Remarks
11.	How does the documented QMS ensure that product conforms to specified requirements?			
12.	Who is responsible for ensuring that the company's Quality Manual meets the requirements of the specified standard for the QMS and does it?			
13.	Do the procedures generated as part of the QMS meet the requirements of the Quality Manual?			
14.	How does the QMS ensure that adequate resources are available to attain and maintain the level of quality detailed in the Quality Manual and/or any Quality Plans?			
15.	How does the QMS identify and ensure that new ideas and techniques that affect quality are verified before being introduced?			
16.	Who is responsible for Identifying requirements and risks that are on the frontiers of company or known technology, how are they controlled and how are new procedures generated if required?			

QMS *Continued*

Item	Requirement	Currently met? Yes/No	Document	Remarks
17.	Who is responsible for clarifying or defining quality standards for the acceptability of product and how are these levels demonstrated?			
18.	How is the compatibility of procedures supporting the QMS established and maintained through revisions?			
19.	How does the QMS exercise continuous and adequate control over areas affecting quality?			
20.	Are written procedures in all areas of the QMS unambiguous, understandable (simple enough so that the intended user has sufficient guidance to assure that quality is maintained) and do they specify methods and criteria?			
21.	Who has the authority to make decisions on the acceptability of the levels of quality achieved?			
22.	How is the QMS represented in contract and new product developments?			
23.	When is the need for a Quality Plan identified, who produces it and how are the contents validated?			

3. Contract Review

Item	Requirement	Currently met? Yes/No	Document	Remarks
24.	Are there procedures for contract review, and are the records readily available and complete?			
25.	Who reviews the contract documents for adequacy and are problem areas resolved?			
26.	Who generates and controls contract-specific procedures and standards and does the customer approve them?			
27.	How are the activities leading up to a tender presentation or quotation co-ordinated?			
28.	Who generates the tender specification and are they aware of all pertinent information?			
29.	Are order acceptance meetings held and, if so, who attends them?			
30.	How are key project personnel identified and informed of their role in the contract?			

Contract Review *Continued*

Item	Requirement	Currently met? Yes/No	Document	Remarks
31.	What evidence is there that the Project Manager has issued all the necessary documentation as detailed in his procedures and was it issued in a timely manner?			
32.	How are verbal orders handled?			
33.	How are the differences between the tender and the contract identified and reviewed?			
34.	How are the in-house activities affecting the customer co-ordinated and agreed with the customer, before and during the contract?			
35.	Do the same procedures apply to all contracts and is this evident?			

4. Design Control

Item	Requirement	Currently met? Yes/No	Document	Remarks
36.	Do procedures exist to control and verify the design activities to ensure the design requirements are specified and met?			
37.	What method of design planning is used and does it identify the need for personnel and equipment that are required?			
38.	How is the requirement for design documentation identified and does this take into consideration the need for training?			
39.	Are there any examples of revised design plans and, if so, why were they modified?			
40.	Who receives and reviews documentation from other departments, the customer, Technical Authority (national safety requirements) affecting the design requirements and what action is taken if the information is unclear or ambiguous?			
41.	Are conflicts and additions to the initial design specification resolved with the person responsible for generating the requirement and, if so, how are unresolved issues progressed?			
42.	How are changes to the design specification and documentation communicated to other departments?			

Design Control *Continued*

Item	Requirement	Currently met? Yes/No	Document	Remarks
43.	Who is responsible for defining and subsequently updating the distribution list for design documentation?			
44.	Is the design specification broken down into smaller units of work and, if so, how are the units related to ensure adequacy when integrated into the whole?			
45.	How is the design validated (tested) to ensure that it performs as specified and are these tests traceable to the customer requirements or national standards?			
46.	Are the design results reviewed and, if so, are they planned and documented?			
47.	If design review meetings are held, who attends them and what evidence is there that a critical review of the results was carried out?			
48.	How are unacceptable test results identified and what action is taken to resolve the situation?			
49.	Where external test houses are required to perform validation, how are they selected, the test specified and the results formatted?			

No.	Question				
50.	Are suitably qualified and experienced personnel assigned to the validation of design?				
51.	Where do the design change requests originate from, how are they reviewed, and are affected documents quarantined until a decision is taken as to the required action to be taken?				
52.	How are approved design changes incorporated into the relevant documentation and are those who need to know informed of the pending changes?				
53.	How is the effect of introducing a design change on the product specification assessed to ensure that no degradation of its performance is introduced?				
54.	How are superseded design documents identified and removed from other relevant areas?				
55.	How are necessary design changes affecting the contract agreed with the customer and, if so, at what point does this happen?				
56.	When are customer-specific standards identified and who controls them and are they available for the use of the designer?				
57.	Are members of the design function aware of the procedures and standards that they should be using and, if so, how can they identify the correct issue?				

Design Control *Continued*

Item	Requirement	Currently met? Yes/No	Document	Remarks
58.	Are suitably qualified and experienced staff allocated to the design and verification activities?			
59.	How are products/documents requiring final approval or certification identified for the company or customer use?			
60.	When was the design documentation as detailed in the procedures produced and has it all been adequately controlled?			
61.	How are completed designs identified and are there any methods of identifying the product status?			
62.	Has adequate documentation been produced to support the product during its expected life and how is this requirement specified?			
63.	Who is responsible for setting design standards and specifications and are all those who need to know aware of these requirements?			
64.	What opportunities are there for designers to assess the requirements and capabilities of the functions that will realise their design and are they aware of what they are?			

5. Document & Data Control

Item	Requirement	Currently met? Yes/No	Document	Remarks
65.	What procedures define how the documents defined in quality requirements are controlled?			
66.	Who reviews and approves the documents for adequacy and are they suitably trained, experienced, and equipped to do so?			
67.	With whose authority is the document approved?			
68.	How are the original and subsequent versions of the document distributed, is its receipt acknowledged and should it be?			
69.	When are copies of obsolete documents destroyed and by whom? Check to ensure that only the authorised issue is available for use			
70.	How are changes to the document implemented, recorded and approved, and is the approval authority the same as for the original issue?			
71.	In approving the document, is the approval authority using recorded information on past experience and, if so, what proof is there?			

Document & Data Control *Continued*

Item	Requirement	Currently met? Yes/No	Document	Remarks
72.	How does the user of the document know what the current version should be?			
73.	Where are the master documents stored and are there any unauthorised modifications?			
74.	Who is responsible for the master document?			
75.	If the document is derived from a standard format, who is responsible for it and do all the users know how to request a change?			
76.	Is the document reissued after every change has been included or, if not, who decides when the document will be reissued and is this time period acceptable to the user of the document?			
77.	Who prepares and updates procedures, who authorises the issue date?			

78.	How does the documentation system make sure that the relevant information is available for the Inspector (or relevant authority) for verification when he needs it?						
79.	How are customer requests to change documents reviewed and recorded?						
80.	Who co-ordinates changes to project documentation, is there only one person responsible and, if not, is the route clearly defined?						
81.	When are changes to the contracted scope of work reviewed and by whom?						
82.	How are the changes to the design, which affect the initial requirements, reviewed and what mechanism is there to ensure that these are in the customer's interest?						
83.	How is the use of superseded documentation controlled and is there any confusion as to what the issue is?						
84.	Who establishes the correct revision of a document if the current issue is not to be used?						
85.	Who is responsible for ensuring that quality documentation is available and issued to the relevant work areas in the appropriate form and in time?						

6.   Purchasing

Item	Requirement	Currently met? Yes/No	Document	Remarks
86.	How are the acceptance criteria for the product performance defined to ensure that it meets specified requirements?			
87.	How are prospective suppliers assessed with respect to quality and other requirements? What are they?			
88.	Who keeps records of supplier performance and are these records available for purchasing decisions?			
89	What action is taken if a non-approved supplier is selected for an order?			
90.	What data is included on the Purchase Order and does it meet customer and company requirements?			
91.	Who reviews the Purchase Order to ensure that it adequately specifies the product?			
92.	Who determines the quality standards to be defined for the order?			

93.	Who is responsible for approving the Purchase Order before release to the supplier and is this value dependent?				
94.	When does the requirement to verify products during manufacture get defined on the Purchase Order?				
95.	How are any validation stages notified to the company and who ensures that the relevant testing is performed before progressing with manufacture?				
96.	What methods exist for the customer to specify and carry out his own inspection?				
97.	How are amendments to the Purchase Orders controlled and authorised and what reference is made to the initial Purchase Order?				
98.	How are designs or other requirement changes communicated to suppliers and are these instructions clear?				
99.	What routes are available for suppliers to resolve queries and what method of progress is used?				
100.	What procedures cover the purchasing activities?				

7. Control of Customer Supplied Product

Item	Requirement	Currently met? Yes/No	Document	Remarks
101.	Who verifies that purchaser (customer) supplied products are fit for the purpose and what method of validation is used and has it been specified?			
102.	Who determines whether specific instructions are required for the maintenance of purchaser supplied products during storage and how are the instructions implemented?			
103.	Where are products that fail to meet specified requirements stored and how are they identified?			
104.	Who prepares specific project instructions for the testing of customer supplied products?			
105.	If there are no written instructions for testing, how is the product validated?			

106.	How are inspections of stored items recorded and who receives them and reviews them to ensure that unsatisfactory test results are analysed and action taken to resolve the situations?		
107.	How are purchaser-supplied products stored and are they segregated to identify those that are not fit for use?		
108.	Are products reinspected prior to use and, if not, how is the product validated to ensure that it is still satisfactory for use?		
109.	Who resolves problems with the customer with respect to products which are unfit or are not available for use? What records are kept?		
110.	Have special storage and inspections been specified by the customer and how can you be sure that these are correct and adequate?		

8. Product Identification and Traceability

Item	Requirement	Currently met? Yes/No	Document	Remarks
111.	Are products clearly identified at all stages of the process?			
112.	How are products in storage identified?			
113.	How are visually identical parts with different characteristics identified?			
114.	Who determines the need to identify products and are instructions issued to define what the products should be traceable to?			
115.	How are the requirements for traceability recorded and are the instructions explicit?			
116.	How are the requirements for traceability on a product/batch which may cause the loss of life, serious injury or loss of production determined, who is assigned this responsibility and are they suitably trained and experienced?			
117.	How is the batch/product marked to ensure that it is uniquely identified and do all associated documents carry the same reference?			
118.	How is traceability assured throughout the life of the product?			

9. Process Control

Item	Requirement	Currently met? Yes/No	Document	Remarks
119.	When are the production/installation processes that need to be controlled, in order to assure the required level of quality, identified?			
120.	Who is responsible for these processes and can they demonstrate that adequate validation and verification takes place to ensure correct manufacturer?			
121.	Who identifies the need for WIs and are they responsible for updating them to take into account new working practices and techniques?			
122.	Where are the WIs filed, are they under control and are the people who are expected to use them aware of them?			
123.	Who has been nominated to ensure that the finished product meets its process requirements and does he have detailed acceptance criteria for assessing the work?			
124.	Who is responsible for ensuring that workmanship standards are adequate to process new or modified products?			

Process Control *Continued*

Item	Requirement	Currently met? Yes/No	Document	Remarks
125.	What reference is made to workmanship standards in instructions?			
126.	When the end product of a process can neither be verified nor validated at its completion, do procedures exist in order to accept it during work in progress and what records are available to prove this?			
127.	Who identifies the need for a special manufacturing process and has he adequately defined it?			
128.	Who is responsible for discussing special processes with the customer/supplier before an order is accepted or placed?			
129.	If the process requires a controlled environment, who has specified its acceptance limits and has it been documented and controlled to these requirements?			
130.	Have the people who have been assigned process duties been adequately equipped to perform the task and is there sufficient space to carry out the work?			

Item	Requirement			
131.	How is reprocessing controlled, and does it follow the same process or do other WIs apply?			
132.	How can you show that the WIs, build documentation and other manufacturing data are at the correct issue and are there any unauthorised additions?			
133.	How are design or specification changes controlled and implemented?			
134.	What systems are in place for ensuring adequate maintenance of production equipment?			

10. Inspection and Testing

Item	Requirement	Currently met? Yes/No	Document	Remarks
135.	Have procedures been generated to ensure that incoming products are verified before being released for use?			
136.	Who inspects or otherwise tests the performance of incoming product before approving it for use and are they aware of the required acceptance criteria?			

Inspection and Testing *Continued*

Item	Requirement	Currently met? Yes/No	Document	Remarks
137.	How are acceptance criteria specified and is there adequate equipment to ensure that these are met?			
138.	How are items, which are not verified, marked?			
139.	How are items, which do not need to be verified, identified and if they subsequently fail, what mechanism is available to recall them for verification?			
140.	How is the past performance of suppliers recorded and is it available for the person taking a decision on the need to validate the incoming product?			
141.	What is done with incoming documentation to substantiate that the product meets specified requirements?			
142.	How are inspection and tests points for work in progress identified and who carries out the validation?			
143.	Who monitors manufacturing processes to ensure that the equipment is fit for purpose and how is this implemented?			

144.	Who is responsible for identifying products that fail to meet their specified requirements and how are these controlled?							
145.	What mechanism is there to ensure that all specified tests have been performed and that the results are acceptable?							
146.	How are the requirements for final inspection and test specified?							
147.	Who verifies that completed products are fit for use?							
148.	How are test and inspection records held and are they accessible and do they meet any contractual and legal requirements?							
149.	Are the people assigned to the validation and verification adequately trained and equipped?							
150.	When appropriate, do all test and inspection records carry the signature or initials of the person performing the validation?							
151.	How does the person carrying out the inspection or test know what documentation he needs and its relevant issue?							
152.	Where relevant, have all test and inspection methods been adequately defined?							

11.   Control of Inspection, Measuring & Test Equipment

Item	Requirement	Currently met? Yes/No	Document	Remarks
153.	Who determines that measuring or test equipment is to be calibrated and how are acceptance limits established and documented?			
154.	Who decides the period of validity for the calibration and is there any provision for subsequently changing it based on past records?			
155.	How is equipment used for indicating rather than measuring identified and has it been calibrated?			
156.	How are the measurement requirements specified and, if appropriate, is the type of test equipment specified in instructions?			
157.	How is the measurement uncertainty specified and are operators aware of what this should be for the work being carried out?			
158.	How is the national standard to which the equipment is to be calibrated specified and, if no suitable standard exists, how is it specified?			
159.	Who is responsible for ensuring that new or reclassified equipment is included in a calibration schedule and how is he informed?			

No.	Question								
160.	What action will be taken if an item sent for calibration fails to meet the specified requirements?								
161.	Where appropriate, is it possible to identify the calibration status of inspection equipment used to demonstrate the adequacy of the product?								
162.	How is it possible to identify the test or inspection equipment used to demonstrate the adequacy of the product?								
163.	How is equipment not needing calibration identified, is it ever used to demonstrate the acceptability of products?								
164.	Who is responsible for ensuring that all calibrated equipment is maintained and stored in a suitable environment so as not to invalidate the calibration?								
165.	Have any special control conditions been defined for calibrated equipment and should it be used under environmentally controlled conditions?								
166.	How is the calibrated equipment checked prior to use to ensure that it is fit for the intended purpose?								
167.	How are adjustments, which can negate the validity of the calibration results, be set or identified to prevent unauthorised adjustments?								
168.	What procedures are in place to control the management and calibration of inspection, measuring and test equipment?								

12. Inspection and Test Status

Item	Requirement	Currently met? Yes/No	Document	Remarks
169.	What method of identification is used to identify the inspection or test status of a product and does it provide adequate information?			
170.	Have all the specified inspections/tests been carried out and who has performed them and are they suitably authorised to do so?			
171.	Where are test and inspection records stores and are they easily traceable to the product?			
172.	Who has the authority to remove a test or inspection indicator?			
173.	Have detailed instructions with respect to defining the status been written?			
174.	Who is responsible for defining the acceptable test status?			
175.	Has provision been made for entering a new status as a result of retesting/inspecting the product?			
176.	What methods of indicating product status are used by suppliers and are they acceptable?			

13. Control of Nonconforming Product

Item	Requirement	Currently met? Yes/No	Document	Remarks
177.	How are products, which do not meet their specified requirement, identified?			
178.	What environment is the nonconforming product stored in and is the marking adequate?			
179.	What documentation is available to identify where the product fails to meet specified requirements?			
180.	Who is responsible for reviewing the documentation in order to recommend a remedial action?			
181.	Whilst a decision is being taken, how are other products, which may also fail to meet specified requirements, identified and segregated and are they?			
182.	What procedures define the control of a nonconforming product process?			
183.	How is remedial action documented and can the product be identified to any such document?			
184.	How are nonconforming products, which are reworked, identified and processed and how can you tell?			

Control of Nonconforming Product *Continued*

Item	Requirement	Currently met? Yes/No	Document	Remarks
185.	Where no remedial action is possible and the product must be disposed of, how is this accomplished and is the routine adequate to prevent further use?			
186.	If the product is reclassified or accepted as is, how is this documented and is the status of the product obvious?			
187.	Are written instructions available as to the required acceptance criteria of the reworked product and how do the revised tests/inspections get recorded?			
188.	When nonconformity affects the customer or other suppliers, how are they involved in the decision taking and approval process?			
189.	How do departments carry out an in-depth consideration of major items which fail to meet specified requirements and who decides what is a major item?			
190.	When are records of nonconforming products reviewed to determine any trends and is there any evidence to support this?			
191.	Where do nonconformance reports go for investigation?			
192.	How effective is the corrective action and is it adequate?			

14. Corrective and Preventive Action

Item	Requirement	Currently met? Yes/No	Document	Remarks
193.	Who investigates the cause of nonconformity and the subsequent actions taken?			
194.	Who is responsible for ensuring that potential causes of nonconformity are identified and action taken to ensure that recurrences do not take place?			
195.	How are customer complaints handled and is there a method of routeng them for analysis by the company's nominated authority?			
196.	How are corrective actions controlled and is the method of control adequately defined?			
197.	What system is available to update procedures to ensure that nonconformities are rectified and preventive measures introduced and are all people who need to be aware of it informed?			
198.	How are changes to methods implemented and recorded?			
199.	What procedures control the processes of Corrective Action and Preventive Action, and what records are available?			

15. Handling, Storage, Packaging, Preservation and Delivery

Item	Requirement	Currently met? Yes/No	Document	Remarks
200.	Who identifies the requirements for handling, storage and packaging and how are they specified?			
201.	Who is responsible for ensuring that the handling, storage and packaging requirements are met and if any validation is required, how is it done?			
202.	How can damage due to inappropriate handling or storage be detected and have procedures been written to ensure that periodic reinspection, when required, is carried out to ensure fitness for purpose?			
203.	Where a storage area has been set up, do methods of receiving and despatching products exist and are all relevant staff knowledgeable?			
204.	How is the product authorised to enter and leave the storage areas?			

205.	Does the product maintain its identity at all stages of handling, storage, packing and delivery and is there evidence to support this?				
206.	Who specifies packaging standards, are there any specific contract requirements and who is responsible for the final packing?				
207.	How are environmental conditions considered when determining requirements to ensure the preservation of quality?				
208.	Who defines the path for the processing of the product and do these instructions define all the relevant processes to be followed?				
209.	Who is responsible for stores records and do they adequately define the current stock holding?				
210.	How are different batches or versions of the same product identified, stored, packed and delivered and is there any scope for confusion?				

16. Control of Records

Item	Requirement	Currently met? Yes/No	Document	Remarks
211.	Which procedures define the need to keep records to demonstrate the achievement of quality determined?			
212.	Who is responsible for generating quality records and is the method of control adequately defined in instructions?			
213.	Does the information on the quality record conform to the requirement as defined in the procedures and, if not, how does it deviate?			
214.	Where quality records are required to be compiled by suppliers to demonstrate their achievement of quality, how is this requirement specified and met?			
215.	Where are quality records kept, for how long, and is the environment suitable to prevent loss or degradation?			
216.	How are quality records accessed and is it possible to analyse them in order to identify trends?			

217.	Who defines for how long the quality record should be kept and does this period conflict with any contractual or legal requirements?		
218.	How can it be demonstrated that the retention of quality records show that the QMS is effective?		
219.	What system is available in order to pass quality records to the customer when required to demonstrate the achievement of quality?		
220.	Who is responsible for disposing of quality records and are they disposed of effectively?		

17. Internal Quality Audits

Item	Requirement	Currently met? Yes/No	Document	Remarks
221.	How effective is the QMS and can this be demonstrated?			
222.	How are audits planned and programmed?			
223.	Does the programme cover the whole QMS?			

Internal Quality Audits *Continued*

Item	Requirement	Currently met? Yes/No	Document	Remarks
224.	How are the requirements for an audit defined and are these instructions supported by procedures?			
225.	Who determines the need for an audit and on what basis do they reach their decision?			
226.	What action is taken after an audit?			
227.	How are nonconformities found during an audit resolved, and are the relevant managers involved?			
228.	How are audit reports controlled and are they circulated to the relevant managers?			
229.	How can the QMS identify that timely corrective actions are taken as a result of an audit?			
230.	When the corrective action is not effective, who is responsible for resolving the situation?			

231.	How are auditors selected and are they suitably trained to carry out an audit?						
232.	Are all auditors independent of the activity that they are auditing and how can this be demonstrated?						
233.	When carrying out the audit, how are the following assessed: structure, personnel, material, resources and product of the activity and are they?						
234.	How are the results of the audit programme reviewed?						
235.	How does the audit programme demonstrate that the QMS is effective?						
236.	Who is responsible for compiling and distributing a 'close out report'?						
237.	How, if at all, are the results of previous audits used to structure the audit of the same or similar function?						
238.	Who is responsible for setting the period between audits and are these periods flexed as a result of past performance or inferred nonconformance identified whilst auditing other activities?						

18.   Training

Item	Requirement	Currently met? Yes/No	Document	Remarks
239.	Who sets the qualification and experience requirements for job functions and in which procedure are they defined?			
240.	Where personnel performing job functions do not meet the identified requirements, how are their training needs identified?			
241.	Having identified the need for training, who is responsible for training and who is responsible for ensuring that these needs are met?			
242.	Who is responsible for ensuring that records of qualification and experience are maintained to reflect the current qualifications and experience of personnel?			

243	How are the training needs of new recruits identified? What training is given on commencement of employment and is it adequate?				
244.	When personnel are redeployed, are they given adequate training in order to perform their new function?				
245.	Are all personnel, on a need to know basis, aware of the QMS and are they aware of how to suggest changes to it?				
246.	Are all levels of management aware of the company's policies affecting their functions and specifically what the company's policy with respect to quality is?				
247.	Who is responsible for reviewing records of qualification to ensure that any new training needs are identified?				

19. Servicing

Item	Requirement	Currently met? Yes/No	Document	Remarks
248.	Who is responsible for ensuring that servicing meets specified requirements and how is this achieved?			
249.	What procedures exist to define the manner of servicing and reporting?			
250.	Who is responsible for generating instructions to ensure that the servicing or after-sales support is adequately defined and who is responsible for ensuring that this information is in a suitable format for the use?			
251.	Who is responsible for providing that adequate back-up is available to ensure that installed and accepted equipment is supported?			
252.	How are requests for support on sites handled, and are all queries responded to in a timely manner?			
253.	How is feedback from servicing handled and how is this feedback co-ordinated?			

20. Statistical Techniques

Item	Requirement	Currently met? Yes/No	Document	Remarks
254.	Who determines the need to use statistical methods to determine the level of quality achieved and are the methods directly related to a standard?			
255.	Who is responsible for gathering data for statistical techniques, is the amount of data specified and is this what is collected?			
256.	Who processes the data and are statistics produced in a timely manner, reviewed and analysed so as to provide an indication of the situation?			
257.	How are statistical data and results controlled and is it adequate?			
258.	Who is responsible for reviewing the statistical techniques and the method of data collection?			
259.	Who has documented the methods of statistical techniques being used?			
260.	Who is responsible for ensuring that the statistical techniques in use are suitable?			
261.	What procedures define the manner of application of statistical techniques?			

3.11 A selection of HEC forms

FORM HEC QA/1

ANNUAL QUALITY AUDIT SCHEDULE FOR THE YEAR ....

APPROVED BY: ....   DATE: ....   ISSUE NO: ....
PAGE .... OF ....

FUNCTION/DEPARTMENT	DOCUMENT REFERENCES	JAN	FEB	MAR	APR	MAY	JUN	JULY	AUG	SEPT	OCT	NOV	DEC

KEY:

INSERT AUDIT NUMBER = AUDIT PLANNED

AUDIT COMPLETE NO CAR

CAR RAISED WAITING FOLLOW-UP

FOLLOW-UP COMPLETE

FORM HEC QA/2
INTERNAL AUDIT PLAN

AUDIT REFERENCE NO: .... DATE OF REQUEST: ....

Purpose of audit: ....

Scope of audit: ....

Lead Auditor assigned: ....

Location(s) of audit: ....

Unit or area to be audited: ....

Reference documents: ....

Team members: ....

Date of audit: ....

Anticipated duration
of audit: ....

Time of opening
meeting: ....

Anticipated time of closing
meeting: ....

Facilities requested: ....

AUDIT REQUEST AUTHORISATION	AUDIT REPORT DISTRIBUTION
	Auditee: ....
Print name:	Lead Auditor: ....
Signature:	File copy: ....

FORM HEC QA/3
PROVISIONAL AUDIT PROGRAMME

FOR: ....

DATE: ....

TIMETABLE	TEAM A	TEAM B	AUDITEE PARTICIPATION
0900–0930	Opening meeting		Senior management and department heads
0930–1030	Managing Director Quality Policy Management Review	Laboratory 1	Technical Director
1030–1100	Review of: Document Control Nonconformity	Laboratory 2	Department Heads
1100–1200	Purchasing	Laboratory 2	Department Heads
1200	Lunch		
1330–1500	Purchasing	Laboratory 2 (cont.)	Department Heads
1500–1600	Personnel Training	Electrical Test House	Department Heads
1600–1700	Commercial/ Sales	Calibration Service	Department Heads

FORM HEC QA/4

AUDIT CHECKLIST

AUDIT CHECKLIST	FUNCTION/PROCESS AUDITED:		AUDIT NO: ....
	DOCUMENT REFERENCES:		AUDIT DATE: ....
ITEM NO	AUDIT QUESTIONS	REFERENCE	RESULT	NOTES/ OBSERVATIONS
PREPARED BY:		PAGE .... OF.........		DATE PREPARED: ....

FORM HEC QA/5
CORRECTIVE ACTION REQUEST

AUDIT NO: .... CAR LOG NO: .... AUDIT DATE: ....

FUNCTION/PROCESS: ....

AUDITOR: .... AUDITEE: ....

DETAILS OF NONCOMPLIANCE:

SIGNATURE: .... SIGNATURE: ....
AUDITOR   **AUDITEE**

PROPOSED CORRECTIVE   **PROPOSED COMPLETION**
ACTION: **DATE:** ....

APPROVED BY: .... APPROVAL DATE: ....
DEPARTMENT MANAGER

FOLLOW-UP ACTION

CORRECTIVE ACTION: **COMPLETE/INCOMPLETE*   2ND FOLLOW-UP**
(Please enter details)   **EFFECTIVE/INEFFECTIVE*   DATE** ....

SIGNATURE: .... DATE: ....
QA MANAGER/AUDITOR

* Delete as appropriate.

FORM HEC QA/6
AUDIT REPORT

AUDITOR NAME:	**AUDIT NO:** ....
PROCESS/FUNCTION AUDITED:	
REFERENCE DOCUMENTS:	

SUMMARY OF AUDIT:

CAR NO	RELATED AREA/DOCUMENT

COMMENTS

AUDITOR SIGNATURE: .... **DATE:** ....

APPROVED: .... **DATE:** ....
QA MANAGER

FORM HEC QA/7

CAR STATUS LOG FOR YEAR ....

Audit No	Car No	Area/Function or Document Affected	Issued To	Date Issued	Response Required Date	Actual Response Date	Follow-up Date	2nd Follow-up Date	Date Car Closed	Authorised Signature

3.12 ISO 9001:2000 elements covered and outstanding

Clause No.	ISO 9001:2000 Title	Covered (Yes/No)
4	Quality Management System (title only)	
4.1	General requirements	
4.2	Documentation requirements (title only)	
4.2.1	General	
4.2.2	Quality Manual	
4.2.3	Control of documents	
4.2.4	Control of records	
5	Management responsibility (title only)	
5.1	Management commitment	
5.2	Customer focus	
5.3	Quality Policy	
5.4	Planning (title only)	
5.4.1	Quality objectives	
5.4.2	Quality management system planning	
5.5	Responsibility, authority and communication (title only)	
5.5.1	Responsibility and authority	
5.5.2	Management representative	
5.5.3	Internal communication	

ISO 9001:2000 elements covered and outstanding *Continued*

Clause No.	ISO 9001:2000 Title	Covered (Yes/No)
5.6	Management review (title only)	
5.6.1	General	
5.6.2	Review input	
5.6.3	Review output	
6	Resource management (title only)	
6.1	Provision of resources	
6.2	Human resources (title only)	
6.2.1	General	
6.2.2	Competence, awareness and training	
6.3	Infrastructure	
6.4	Work environment	
7	Product realisation (title only)	
7.1	Planning of product realisation	
7.2	Customer-related processes (title only)	
7.2.1	Determination of requirements related to the product	
7.2.2	Review of requirements related to the product	
7.2.3	Customer communication	
7.3	Design and development (title only)	
7.3.1	Design and development planning	

ISO 9001:2000 elements covered and outstanding *Continued*

Clause No.	ISO 9001:2000 TItle	Covered (Yes/No)
7.3.2	Design and development inputs	
7.3.3	Design and development outputs	
7.3.4	Design and development review	
7.3.5	Design and development verification	
7.3.6	Design and development validation	
7.3.7	Control of design and development changes	
7.4	Purchasing (title only)	
7.4.1	Purchasing process	
7.4.2	Purchasing information	
7.4.3	Verification of purchased product	
7.5	Production and service provision (title only)	
7.5.1	Control of production and service provision	
7.5.2	Validation of processes for production and service provision	
7.5.3	Identification and traceability	
7.5.4	Customer property	
7.5.5	Preservation of product	
7.6	Control of monitoring and measuring devices	
8	Measurement, analysis and improvement (title only)	
8.1	General	

ISO 9001:2000 elements covered and outstanding *Continued*

Clause No.	ISO 9001:2000 Title	Covered (Yes/No)
8.2	Monitoring and measurement (title only)	
8.2.1	Customer satisfaction	
8.2.2	Internal audit	
8.2.3	Monitoring and measurement of processes	
8.2.4	Monitoring and measurement of product	
8.3	Control of nonconforming product	
8.4	Analysis of data	
8.5	Improvement (title only)	
8.5.1	Continual improvement	
8.5.2	Corrective action	
8.5.3	Preventive action	

3.13 Abbreviations and acronyms

AFNOR	Association Francais de Normalisation
ANSI	American National Standards Institute
AQAP	Allied Quality Assurance Publications (NATO)
ASQ	American Society for Quality (was ASQC)
ASQC	American Society for Quality Control (now ASQ)
ASTM	American Society for Testing and Materials
BS	British Standard, issued by BSI
BSI	British Standards Institution
CCIR	International Radio Consultative Committee
CCITT	The International Telegraph and Telephony Consultative Committee
CECC	CENELEC Electronic Components Committee
CEN	Commission European de Normalisation
CENELEC	European Committee for Electrotechnical Standardisation
COS	Corporation of Open Systems
CP	Core Process
CSA	Canadian Standards Association
DIN	Deutsches Institut für Normung (German Institute for Standardisation)
DIS	Draft International Standard
DTI	Department of Trade and Industry
DOD	(American) Division of Defense
EEC	European Economic Community
EMS	Environmental Management System
EN	European Normalisation (the number for European standards)
EN HD	European Harmonised Directive
EU	European Union
FDIS	Final Draft International Standard
FIIE(elec)	Fellow of the Institution of Electronics and Electrical Incorporated Engineers
FinstM	Fellow of the Institute of Management
IAF	International Accreditation Forum
IEC	International Electrotechnical Commission
IEE	Institution of Electrical Engineers
IQA	Institute of Quality Assurance
ISO	International Organisation for Standardisation
ISO/CASCO	OSI Committee on Conformity Testing
ISO/TC176	The ISO Technical Committee responsible for the ISO 9000 series standards
IT	Information Technology
ITU	International Telecommunications Union
MIQA	Member of the Institute of Quality Assurance

MIRSE	Member of the Institution of Railway Signal Engineers
MSc	Master of Science
MTBF	Mean Time Between Failures
NQIC	National Quality Information Centre
NSA	National Supervising Authority
NSO	National Standards Organisation
OSI	Open Systems Connection
PF	Probability Function
QA	Quality Assurance
QAI	Quality Assurance Inspector
QC	Quality Control
QM	Quality Manual
QMS	Quality Management System
QP	Quality Procedure
SP	Supporting Processes
TQM	Total Quality Management (BS 7850)
UK	United Kingdom
VDE	Verband Deutsch Elektrotechniker
WI	Work Instruction

3.14 Glossary of terms used in quality

As international trade increases, it is becoming more important than ever to know the exact meaning of some of the basic definitions when referred to the quality of a product or service – especially when used in the vernacular. To overcome this problem an international standard (ISO 8402:1994 – Quality management and quality assurance – vocabulary) was published in three languages (English, French and Russian).

ISO 9000:2000 was then developed within ISO/TC 176. It was developed by first screening existing quality standards (e.g. ISO 8402:1994) and publications that were available to determine the quality terms that could be included and then producing internationally acceptable definitions of them. Because of this 'international acceptability' many of these definitions and terms have specific meanings and applications as opposed to generic definitions that are normally to be found in dictionaries.

Acceptance: Agreement to take a product or service as offered.

Accreditation: Certification, by a duly recognised body, of facilities, capability, objectivity, competence and integrity of an agency, service or operational group or individual to provide the specific service/s or operation/s as needed.

Audit: Systematic, independent and documented process for obtaining evidence and evaluating it objectively to determine the extent to which audit criteria are fulfilled.

Audit client: Person or organisation requesting an audit.

Audit conclusions: Outcome of an audit decided by the audit team after consideration of all the audit findings.

Audit criteria: Set of policies, procedures or requirements against which collected audit evidence is compared.

Audit evidence: Records, verified statements of fact or other information relevant to the audit.

Audit findings: Results of the evaluation of the collected audit evidence against audit criteria.

Audit programme: Set of audits to be carried out during a planned time frame.

Audit scope: Extent and range of a given audit.

Audit team: One or more auditors conducting an audit, one of whom is appointed as leader.

Auditee: Organisation being audited.

Auditor: Person qualified and competent to conduct audits.

Bonded store: A secure place in which only supplies that have been accepted as satisfactory by the inspection staff are held.

Calibration: The operation that is required to determine the accuracy of measuring and test equipment.

Capability: Ability of an organisation, system or process to realise a product that fulfils the requirements for that product.

Cen (European Committee for Standardisation): European equivalent of ISO.

Cenelec (European Committee for Electrotechnical Standardisation) Certification Body: An impartial body who have the necessary competence and reliability to operate a certification scheme.

Censored test: A test carried out on a number of items which is terminated before all the tested items have failed.

Certification: The procedure and action by a duly authorised body of determining, verifying and attesting in writing to the qualifications of personnel, processes, procedures, or items in accordance with applicable requirements.

Certification body: An impartial body, governmental or non-governmental, possessing the necessary competence and reliability to operate a certification system, and in which the interests of all parties concerned with the functioning of the system are represented.

Certification system: A system having its own rules of procedure and management for carrying out certification.

Chief inspector: An individual who is responsible for the manufacturer's Quality Management System (also referred to as the Quality Manager).

Company: Term used primarily to refer to a business first party, the purpose of which is to supply a product or service.

Compliance: The fulfilment of a Quality Management System or quality procedure of specified requirements.

Concession: Authorisation to use or release a product that does not conform to specified requirements.

Concession/waiver: Written authorisation to use or release a quantity of material, components or stores already produced but which do not conform to the specified requirements.

Consignment: Products (or goods) that are issued or received as one delivery and covered by one set of documents.

Contract: Agreed requirements between a supplier and customer transmitted by any means.

Corrective action: Action taken to eliminate the cause of a detected nonconformity or other undesirable situation.

Customer: Ultimate consumer, user, client, beneficiary or second party.

Customer complaint: Any written, electronic, or oral communication that alleges deficiencies related to the identity, quality, durability, reliability, safety or performance of a device that has been placed on the market.

Customer dissatisfaction: Customer's opinion of the degree to which a transaction has failed to meet the customer's needs and expectations.

Customer organisation: Customer organisation or person that receives a product.

Customer satisfaction: Customer's opinion of the degree to which a transaction has met the customer's needs and expectations.

Defect: Non-fulfilment of a requirement related to an intended or specified use.

Design and development: Set of processes that transforms requirements into specified characteristics and into the specification of the product realisation process.

Design authority: The approved firm, establishment or branch representative responsible for the detailed design of material to approved specifications and authorised to sign a certificate of design, or to certify sealed drawings.

Design capability: The ability of a manufacturer to translate a customer requirement into a component that can be manufactured by their particular technology.

Design failure: A failure due to an inadequate design of an item.

Design review: A formal, documented, comprehensive and systematic examination of a design to evaluate the design requirements and the capability of the design to meet these requirements and to identify problems and propose solutions.

Document: Information and its support medium.

Effectiveness: Measure of the extent to which planned activities are realised and planned results achieved.

Efficiency: Relationship between the result achieved and the resources used.

Environment: All of the external physical conditions that may influence the performance of a product or service.

Environmental condition: The characteristics (such as humidity, pressure, vibration etc.) of the environment in which the product is operating.

Equipment: Machines, apparatus, fixed or mobile devices, control components and instrumentation thereof and detection or prevention systems which, separately or jointly, are intended for the generation, transfer, storage, measurement, control and conversion of energy for the processing of material and which are capable of causing an explosion through their own potential sources of ignition.

Evaluation: The systematic evaluation of the effectiveness of a contractor's Quality Management System.

Failure: The termination of the ability of an item to perform a required function.

Failure mode, effect and criticality analysis (FMECA): FMEA together with a consideration of the probability of occurrence and a ranking of the seriousness of the failure.

Failure mode/fault mode: One of the possible states of a failed (faulty) item, for a given required function.

Failure mode and effect analysis (FMEA): A qualitative method of reliability analysis which involves the study of the failure modes which can exist in every sub-item of the item and the determination of the effects of each failure mode on other sub-items of the item and on the required function of the item.

Failure rate (instantaneous): The limit, if this exists, of the conditional probability that the instant of time of a failure of an item falls within a given time interval to the length of this interval, when given that the item is in an up state at the beginning of the time interval.

Failure tree analysis (FTA): The study, with the use of diagrammatic algorithms, of the possible sequence of events leading up to the failure of a product.

Fault: The state of an item characterised by inability to perform a required function, excluding the inability during preventive maintenance or due to lack of external resources or other planned action.

Fault tree: A logic diagram showing how a given fault mode of an item is related to possible fault modes of sub-items or to external events, or combinations thereof.

Fault tree analysis: An analysis in the form of a fault tree in order to determine how a stated fault mode of the item may be the result of the fault modes of the sub-items or of external events, or combinations thereof.

Final inspection: The last inspection by a manufacturer or supplier before delivery.

In-process inspection: Inspection carried out at various stages during processing.

In-progress inspections: QA Inspectors perform these on a random basis or while assisting the technician. They may also be considered as 'training' inspections and are meant to help the technician perform better maintenance whilst actually learning about the equipment.

Inspection: Activities such as measuring, examining, testing, gauging one or more characteristics of a product or service and comparing these with specified requirements to determine conformity.

Interested party: Person or group having an interest in the performance or success of an organisation.

Maintenance: The combination of technical and administrative actions that are taken to retain or restore an item to a state in which it can perform its stated function.

Management: Co-ordinated activities to direct and control an organisation.

Management system: To establish policy and objectives and to achieve those objectives.

Manufacturer: The natural or legal person with responsibility for the design, manufacture, packaging and labelling of a device before it is placed on the market under his own name, regardless of whether these operations are carried out by that person himself or on his behalf by a third party.

May: This auxiliary verb indicates a course of action often followed by manufacturers and suppliers.

Measurement: Set of operations having the object of determining the value of a quantity.

Nonconformity: Non-fulfilment of a requirement.

Operational cycle: A repeatable sequence of functional stresses.

Operational requirements: All the function and performance require- ments of a product.

Organisation: A company, corporation, firm or enterprise, whether incorporated or not, public or private.

Group of people and facilities with an orderly arrangement of responsibilities, authorities and relationships.

Organisational structure: Orderly arrangement of responsibilities, authorities and relationships between people.

Outgoing inspections: These are performed after a job or task has been completed to verify that everything has been done correctly on a repaired equipment that is ready for return to the customer. The Quality Assurance Inspector is normally required to check the item to see how it compares against the manufacturer's specification. Any item failing an outgoing inspection has to be returned to the Technician or his Section Manager for corrective action. It will then be subject to a further outgoing inspection by the QA Inspector.

Procedure: Describes the way to perform an activity or process.

Product: Result of a process.

NOTE There are four agreed generic product categories:

- hardware (e.g. engine mechanical part);
- software (e.g. computer program);
- services (e.g. transport);
- processed materials (e.g. lubricant).

Hardware and processed materials are generally tangible products, while software or services are generally intangible.

Most products comprise elements belonging to different generic product categories. Whether the product is then called hardware, processed material, software or service depends on the dominant element.

Project: Unique process, consisting of a set of co-ordinated and controlled activities with start and finish dates, undertaken to achieve an objective conforming to specific requirements, including the constraints of time, costs and resources.

Quality: Ability of a set of inherent characteristics of a product, system or process to fulfil requirements of customers and other interested parties.

Quality assurance: Part of quality management, focused on providing confidence that quality requirements are fulfilled.

Quality audit: A systematic and independent examination to determine whether quality activities and related results comply with planned arrangements and whether these arrangements are implemented effectively and are suitable to achieve objectives.

Quality control: Part of quality management, focused on fulfilling quality requirements.

Quality costs: The expenditure incurred by the producer, by the user and by the community, associated with product or service quality.

Quality level: A general indication of the extent of the product's departure from the ideal.

Quality loop: Conceptual model of interacting activities that influence the quality of a product or service in the various stages ranging from the identification of needs to the assessment of whether these needs have been satisfied.

Quality manager: A person who is responsible for the manufacturer's Quality Management System (also sometimes referred to as the Chief Inspector).

Quality management: That aspect of the overall management function that determines and implements the quality policy.
   NOTE The terms 'quality management' and 'quality control' are considered to be a manufacturer/supplier (or 1st party) responsibility. 'Quality Assurance' on the other hand has both internal and external aspects which in many instances can be shared between the manufacturer/supplier (1st party), purchaser/customer (2nd party) and any regulatory/certification body (3rd party) that may be involved.

Quality Management System: System to establish a quality policy and quality objectives and to achieve those objectives.

Quality Management System review: A formal evaluation by top management of the status and adequacy of the Quality Management System in relation to quality policy and new objectives resulting from changing circumstances.

Quality manual: Document specifying the quality management system of an organisation.

Quality plan: Document specifying the quality management system elements and the resources to be applied in a specific case.

Quality policy: The overall quality intentions and direction of an organisation as regards quality, as formally expressed by top management.

Quality procedure: A description of the method by which quality system activities are managed.

Quality records: Records should provide evidence of how well the Quality System has been implemented.

Quality system: The organisational structure, responsibilities, procedures, processes and resources for implementing quality management.

Quarantine store: A secure place to store supplies that are awaiting proof that they comply with specified requirements.

Receiving inspection/incoming inspection: Inspection by a customer (or department) of materials and manufactured products as received.

Record: Document stating results achieved or providing evidence of activities performed.

Reliability: The ability of an item to perform a required function under stated conditions for a stated period of time.

Repair: Action taken on a nonconforming product to make it acceptable for the intended usage.

Requirement: Need or expectation that is stated, customarily implied or obligatory.

Review: Activity undertaken to ensure the suitability, adequacy, effectiveness and efficiency of the subject matter to achieve established objectives.

Risk: The combined effect of the probability of occurrence of an undesirable event, and the consequence of the event.

Sample: A group of items or individuals, taken from a larger collection or population that provides information needed for assessing a characteristic (or characteristics) of the population, or which serves as a basis for action on the population, or the process that produced it.

Shall: This auxiliary verb indicates a course of action that must be followed by manufacturers and suppliers.

Should: This auxiliary verb indicates that a certain course of action is preferred but not necessarily required.

Specification: The document that describes the requirements with which the product, material or process has to conform.

Supplier: The organisation that provides a product to the customer (EN ISO 8402:1995).

Note 1. In a contractual situation, the supplier may be called the contractor.

Note 2. The supplier may be, for example, the producer, distributor, importer, assembler or service organisation.

Note 3. The supplier may be either external or internal to the organisation.

Note 4.   With regard to MDD the term supplier is NOT used. The Directive instead refers to 'manufacturer'.

Supplier evaluation: Assessment of a supplier's capability to control quality.

Supplier rating: An index related to the performance of a supplier.

Top management: Person or group of people who direct and control an organisation at the highest level.

User requirement: The documented product or service requirements of a customer or user.

Validation: Confirmation and provision of objective evidence that the requirements for a specific intended use or application have been fulfilled.

Verification: The act of reviewing, inspecting, testing, checking, auditing or otherwise establishing and documenting whether items, processes, services, or documents conform to specified requirements.

Work instruction: A description of how a specific task is carried out.

REFERENCES

Standards

Number	Date	Title
ANSI 90 series		American quality standards
BS 4778–1	1987	Quality vocabulary
BS 4778–2	1979	Quality vocabulary – international terms, national terms
BS 4778–3.1	1991	Quality vocabulary – availability, reliability and maintainability terms – guide to concepts and related definitions
BS 4778–3.2	1991	Quality vocabulary – availability, reliability and maintainability terms – glossary of international terms
BS 4891	1972	A guide to quality assurance
BS 5701	1980	Guide to number defective charts for quality control
BS 5703	1980	Guide to data analysis quality control using cusum charting
BS 5750 series	1987	Quality systems – principal concepts and applications
BS 5750–1	1979	Quality systems – specification for design, development, production, installation and servicing
BS 5750–2	1979	Quality systems – specification for production and installation

Number	Date	Title
BS 5750–3	1979	Quality systems – specification for final inspection and test
BS 6001	1999	Sampling procedures for inspection by attributes
BS 6002	1993	Sampling procedures for inspection by variables
BS 6143–1	1992	Guide to the economics of quality – process cost model
BS 6143–2	1990	Guide to the economics of quality – prevention, appraisal and failure mode
BS 7850–1	1991	Total quality management – guide to management principles
BS 7850–2	1992	Total quality management – guide to quality improvement methods
BS 7850–3	1994	Total quality management – guidelines for quality improvement
BS 8800	1996	Guide to occupational health and safety management systems
EN 29000	1987	Renumbered as ISO 9000/1
ISO 8402	1995	Quality management and quality assurance – vocabulary
ISO 9000		Quality management and quality assurance standards
ISO 9000	2000	Quality Management Systems – fundamentals and vocabulary
ISO 9000–1	1994	Quality management and quality assurance standards – guidelines for selection and use
ISO 9000–2	1997	Quality management and quality assurance standards – generic guidelines for the application of ISO 9001, 9002 and 9003
ISO 9000–3	1997	Quality management and quality assurance standards – guidelines for the application of ISO 9001:1994 to the development, supply, installation and maintenance of computer software

Number	Date	Title
ISO 9000–4	1993	Quality management and quality assurance standards – guide to dependability programme management
ISO 9001	1994	Quality systems – model for quality assurance in design/development, production, installation and servicing
ISO 9001	2000	Quality Management Systems – requirements
ISO 9002	1994	Quality systems – model for quality assurance in production and installation
ISO 9003	1994	Quality systems – model for quality assurance in final inspection and test
ISO 9004		Superseded by ISO 9004–1
ISO 9004	2000	Quality management systems – guidance for performance improvement
ISO 9004–1	1994	Quality management and quality system elements – guidelines
ISO 9004–2	1991	Quality management and quality system elements – guidelines for service
ISO 9004–3	1993	Quality management and quality system elements – guidelines for processed materials
ISO 9004–4	1994	Quality management and quality system elements – guidelines for quality improvement
ISO 10005	1995	Quality management – guidelines for quality plans
ISO 10011–1	1990	Guidelines for auditing quality systems – auditing
ISO 10011–2	1991	Guidelines for auditing quality systems – qualification criteria for quality systems auditors
ISO 10011–3	1991	Guidelines for auditing quality systems – management of audit programmes

Number	Date	Title
ISO 10012–1	1992	Quality assurance requirements for measuring equipment – metrological confirmation system for measuring equipment
ISO 10012–2	1997	Quality assurance for measuring equipment – guidelines for control of measurement processes
ISO 10013	1995	Guidelines for developing quality manuals
ISO 14001	1996	Environmental management systems – specifications with guidance for use
ISO 14010	1996	Guidelines for environmental auditing – general principles
ISO 14011	1996	Guidelines for environmental auditing – auditing procedures – auditing of environmental management systems
ISO 14012	1996	Guidelines for environmental auditing – qualification criteria for environmental auditors
ISO TR 10017	1999	Guidance on statistical techniques for ISO 9001:1994
QS 9000	1995	Quality system requirements (for the automotive industry)
TR 9000		Quality system requirements (for the electronics industry)

Other references

Title	Author	Publisher
Operating degradations during the in-service stage	Tricker, R.L.	StingRay Management Consultants, 1999
Quality – its origin and progress in defence procurement	Drew, H.E.	Paper to the Institution of Production Engineers, 1971
Quality assurance	PSA	HMSO, 1987. ISBN 86177:143.53

Title	Author	Publisher
Quality counts – developments in qualities and standards since 1982	White Paper	HMSO
Quality Management Handbook (BSI)		BSI
Standards, quality and international competitiveness	DTI	October 1986
Standards, quality and international competitiveness	White Paper	Cmnd 8621, July 1982
Statistical process control	Oakland, John	Butterworth-Heinemann, 1986
Working for quality		BSI

NOTES
Extracts from British Standards are reproduced with the permission of the British Standards Institute. Complete copies of all British Standards can be obtained, by post, from Customer Services, BSI Standards, 389 Chiswick High Road, London W4 4AL.

Books by the same author

Title	Details	Publisher
ISO 9001:2000 for Small Businesses (Second Edition)	Fully revised and updated, *ISO 9001:2000 for Small Businesses* explains the new requirements of ISO 9001:2000 and helps businesses draw up a quality plan to allow them to meet the challenges of the marketplace.	Butterworth-Heinemann ISBN: 0 7506 4882 1

Title	Details	Publisher
ISO 9001:2000 in Brief	A 'hands on' book providing practical information on how to cost effectively set up an ISO 9001:2000 Quality Management System.	Butterworth-Heinemann ISBN: 0 7506 4814 7
CE Conformity Marking	Essential information for any manufacturer or distributor wishing to trade in the European Union. Practical and easy to understand.	Butterworth-Heinemann ISBN: 0 7506 4813 9
Environmental Requirements for Electromechanical and Electronic Equipment	Definitive reference containing all the background guidance, ranges, test specifications, case studies and regulations worldwide.	Butterworth-Heinemann ISBN: 0 7506 3902 4
MDD Compliance using Quality Management Techniques	Easy to follow guide to MDD, enabling the purchaser to customise the Quality Management System to suit his own business.	Butterworth-Heinemann ISBN: 0 7506 4441 9
Quality and Standards in Electronics	Ensures that manufacturers are aware of the all the UK, European and international necessities, know the current status of these regulations and standards, and where to obtain them.	Butterworth-Heinemann ISBN: 0 7506 2531 7

USEFUL ADDRESSES

American National Standards Institute (ANSI)

1819 L Street, NW Washington, DC 20036, USA
Tel: 00 1 202 293 8020
Fax: 00 1 202 293 9287
e-mail: ansionline@ansi.org
website: http://www.ansi.org

American Society for Quality Control (ASQ)

611 East Wisconsin Avenue, PO Box 3005
Milwaukee WI 53201–3005, USA
Tel: 00 1 414 272 8575 or 800 248 1946
Fax: 00 1 414 272 1734
e-mail: cs@asq.org
website: http://www.asq.org

British Standards Institution (BSI)

389 Chiswick High Road, London W4 4AL, UK
Tel: 020 8996 9001
Fax: 020 8996 7001
e-mail: info@bsi.org.uk
website: http://www.bsi.org.uk

Comission Europeen de Normalisation (CEN)

36, rue de Stassart, 1050 Bruxelles, Belgium
Tel: 0032 2 550 08 11
Fax: 0032 2 550 08 19
e-mail: infodesk@cenclcbel.be
website: http://www.cenorm.be

ETSI

Route des Lucioles – Sophia Antipolis –
Valbonne 06921, Sophia Antipolis, France
Tel: 0033 4 92 94 42 00
Fax : 0033 4 93 65 47 16
e-mail: infocentre@etsi.fr
website: http://www.etsi.org

European Committee for Electrotechnical Standardisation (CENELEC)

35, rue de Stassart, 1050 Bruxelles, Belgium
Tel: 0032 2 519 68 71
Fax : 0032 2 519 69 19
e-mail: general@cenelec.be
website: http://www.cenelec.be

European Organisation for Testing and Certification (EOTC)	Egmont House, Rue d'Egmont 15, 1000 Bruxelles, Belgium Tel: 0032 2 502 4141 Fax: 0032 2 502 4239
ILI	Index House, Ascot, Berkshire, SL5 7EU, UK Tel: 01344 636400 Fax: 01344 291194 email: databases@ili.co.uk website: www.ili.co.uk
ILI (America)	60 Winters Avenue, Paramus, NJ 07652, USA e-mail: sales@ili-info.com
International Electrotechnical Commission (IEC)	Rue de Varembe 3, Case Postale 131, 1211 Geneva 20, Switzerland Tel: 0041 22 919 0211 Fax: 0041 22 919 0300 website: http://www.iec.ch
International Standards Organisation (ISO)	Case Postal 56, 1222 Geneva 20, Switzerland Tel: 0041 22 749 0336 Fax: 0041 22 734 1079 website: http://www.iso.ch
National Center for Standards and Certification Information	US Department of Commerce, Building 820, Room 164, Gaithersburg, MD 20899, USA Tel: 00 1 301 9754040 EU Hotline: 00 1 301 921–4164 Fax: 00 1 301 926 1559
Office of the Official Publications of the EC	2 Rue Mercier, 2144 Luxembourg Tel: 00352–29291 Fax: 00352 292942763 e-mail: infor.info@opece.cec.be website: http://www.eur-op.eu.int
VDE-Verlag GmbH	Bismarkstrasse 33, 10625 Berlin, Germany Tel: 0049 30 348001–0 Fax: 0049 30 3417093 e-mail: service@vde.com website: http://www.vde.de

Index